Oracle Solid State Disk Tuning
High Performance Oracle tuning with RAM disk

Donald K. Burleson
Mike Ault

RAMPANT
TECHPRESS

We dedicate this book to our friends at Texas Memory Systems whose dedication to this experiment was instrumental in creating this book.

-- Donald K. Burleson

-- Mike Ault

Oracle Solid State Disk Tuning
High Performance Oracle tuning with RAM disk

By Donald K. Burleson and Mike Ault

Copyright © 2004 by Rampant TechPress. All rights reserved.

Printed in the United States of America.

Published by: Rampant TechPress, Kittrell, North Carolina, USA

Oracle In-Focus Series: Book # 7

Editors: John Lavender, Janet Burleson, Kelly Gay and Teri Wade

Production Editor: Teri Wade

Production Manager: Linda Webb

Cover Design: Bryan Hoff

Illustrations: Mike Reed

Printing History:

October 2004 for First Edition

March 2005 for Second Printing

Special thanks to Woody Hutsell for his contributions to this publication.

ISBN: 0-9744486-5-6

Library of Congress Control Number: 2004113187

Table of Contents

Using the Download Depot

Purchase of this book provides complete access to the online quick-reference horse emergency checklists.

All of the scripts in this book are located at the following URL:

www.rampant.cc/ssd.htm

If technical assistance is required in downloading or accessing the download site, please contact Rampant TechPress at info@rampant.cc.

Advanced Oracle Monitoring and Tuning Script Collection

The complete collection from Mike Ault, the world's best DBA.

Packed with 590 ready-to-use Oracle scripts, this is the definitive collection for every Oracle professional DBA.

It would take many years to develop these scripts from scratch, making this download the best value in the Oracle industry.

It's only $39.95 (less than 7 cents per script!)

To buy for immediate download, go to

www.rampant.cc/aultcode.htm

Conventions Used in this Book

It is critical for any technical publication to follow rigorous standards and employ consistent punctuation conventions to make the text easy to read.

However, this is not an easy task. Within Oracle there are many types of notation that can confuse a reader. Some Oracle utilities such as STATSPACK and TKPROF are always spelled in CAPITAL letters, while Oracle parameters and procedures have varying naming conventions in the Oracle documentation. It is also important to remember that many Oracle commands are case sensitive, and are always left in their original executable form, and never altered with italics or capitalization.

Hence, all Rampant TechPress books follow these conventions:

Parameters - All Oracle parameters will be lowercase italics. Exceptions to this rule are parameter arguments that are commonly capitalized (KEEP pool, TKPROF), these will be left in ALL CAPS.

Variables – All PL/SQL program variables and arguments will also remain in lowercase italics (*dbms_job*, *dbms_utility*).

Tables & dictionary objects – All data dictionary objects are referenced in lowercase italics (*dba_indexes*, *v$sql*). This includes all v$ and x$ views (*x$kcbcbh*, *v$parameter*) and dictionary views (*dba_tables*, *user_indexes*).

SQL – All SQL is formatted for easy use in the code depot, and all SQL is displayed in lowercase. The main SQL terms (select, from, where, group by, order by, having) will always appear on a separate line.

Programs & Products – All products and programs that are known to the author are capitalized according to the vendor specifications (IBM, DBXray, etc). All names known by Rampant TechPress to be trademark names appear in this text as initial caps. References to UNIX are always made in uppercase.

Acknowledgements

This type of highly technical reference book requires the dedicated efforts of many people. Even though we are the authors, our work ends when we deliver the content. After each chapter is delivered, experienced copy editors polish the grammar and syntax.

The finished work is then reviewed as page proofs and turned over to the production manager, who arranges the creation of the online code depot and manages the cover art, printing, distribution, and warehousing. In short, the authors played a small role in the development of this book, and we need to thank and acknowledge everyone who helped bring this book to fruition:

Teri Wade, for her hard work formatting the manuscript and producing the page proofs.

Linda Webb, for her production management, including the coordination of the cover art, page proofing, printing, and distribution.

Kelly Gay, for her expert page-proofing services.

Mike Reed, for his superb cartoons.

With our sincere thanks,

Don Burleson & Mike Ault

Preface

Technology is a rapidly changing thing and those who get left behind will suffer the consequences. Almost every year a new technology appears that changes the face of database systems and the advent of Solid-State Disk (SSD) appears to be one of the most important advances in database technology since the introduction of the relational database model.

The advent of SSD is especially important to the Oracle professional because it changes the main tuning paradigm. Whereas the Oracle DBA of the 1990's was concerned with reducing disk I/O latency, this has now been removed with SSD, and the Oracle professional must learn a whole new way to manage and tune their Oracle databases.

In 2004, SSD costs about $1,000 per gigabyte, making it too expensive for large Oracle systems. As such, the focus of this book will be to show you how to apply SSD to where it will do the most good, targeting SSD technology to those areas where your Oracle database will benefit the most.

Of course, in just a few years SSD will as cheap as standard disk today, and the principles set forth in this text will lay the foundation for a whole new generation of Oracle database management.

Until that time, please carefully evaluate the important concepts set-forth in our benchmark study, especially the conclusions and recommendations. Remember, technology is constantly changing, and solid-state Oracle will be a part of your future.

Judging Solid-State Disk with Oracle

CHAPTER

1

Introduction

As a result of living in a world of constantly improving hardware technology, yesterday's mainframe is today's PC. There have been unprecedented improvements to the speed and cost of computer hardware. Moore's Law dictates that hardware costs will constantly fall while prices become constantly cheaper (Figure 1.1).

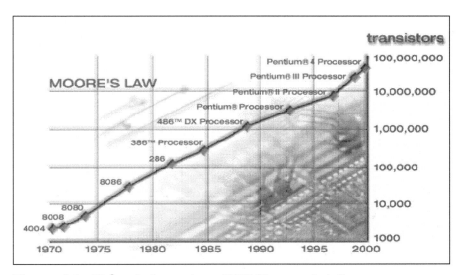

Figure 1.1 - Moore's Law circa 1975 (Source Intel)

This rapid change is especially evident for Random Access Memory (RAM). Using RAM memory is critical to the performance of today's database management systems because RAM speed (expressed in nanoseconds) is more than 10,000 times faster than traditional disk storage device speed (expressed in milliseconds). RAM allows data to be accessed far faster than disk technology, and I/O-bound Oracle systems will soon be able to benefit from RAM like never before.

The latest incarnation of RAM storage devices are the solid-state disk (SSD) technology. With SSD the ancient spinning platters of magnetic-coated media are replaced with an array of super-fast solid-state RAM. Just like disks were backed-up to tape, today's SSD devices write the RAM frames to a back-end disk with software.

With the cost of SSD at only $1,000 per gigabyte, many Oracle systems are exploring how to leverage this powerful performance tool for their environment. Smaller databases can now run fully-cached with SSD, yet there is debate about the proper use of SSD in an Oracle environment.

Some IT managers cry about the high-cost of Solid-state disk

The proper use of SSD is the central question for this benchmark. Traditional architectures of the 1990's have resulted in duplicitous cache areas. For example, web cache, Oracle buffer cache, and on-board disk cache. Now the challenge of the Oracle DBA is to exploit SSD to benefit their database applications.

In the following sections these topics will be covered:

Introduction to data caching – There is an ongoing debate about the effect of data caching, resulting in many opposing theories and conflicting research results. This section will take an objective look at the caching issue for Oracle databases.

Hypothesis – This section will predict what the Oracle SSD benchmark might reveal and justify the basis for the choices of testing scenarios.

Methodology – Describes the Transaction Processing Performance Council (TPC) database environment and the choice of hardware. Complete details are presented in Appendix A.

Results – This section contains the test results.

Conclusions – This section will compare the predicted results with the hypothesis. It also includes an extrapolation of the results and generalizes the benefits of SSD for specific types of Oracle database systems.

Introduction to Oracle data caching

Leveraging RAM resources has always been one of the central tasks of the Database Administrator (DBA). By definition, almost all databases are I/O intensive and minimizing the expensive physical disk I/O has always been a major priority to ensure acceptable performance. Historically, RAM has been a scarce and expensive resource, and the DBA was challenged to find the most-used data to cache on precious RAM media.

However, RAM is quite different from other hardware. Unlike CPU speed, which improves every year, RAM speed is constrained by the physics of silicon technology. Instead of speed improvements, there is a constant decline in price. CPU speed also continues to outpace RAM speed and this means that RAM sub-systems must be localized to keep CPUs running at full capacity.

In the 1980's, 1 gigabyte of RAM cost more than one million dollars whereas today 1 gigabyte of high-speed RAM storage can be obtained for less than $2,000. The following table shows how the cost of RAM has decreased over time:

YEAR	PRICE PER GBYTE TO ADD MEMORY TO SOLID STATE DISK
1998	$9,000 (TMS)
1999	$6,000 (TMS)
2000	$5,000 (TMS)
2001	$5,000 (TMS)
2002	$3,000 (TMS)
2003	$2,500 (TMS)
2004	$1,500 (TMS)

Historically, RAM I/O bandwidth grows one bit every 18 months, making the first decade of the 21st Century the era of 64-bit RAM technology:

1970's	8 bit
1980's	16 bit
1990's	32 bit
2000's	64 bit
2010's	128 bit

These numbers typically have as much to do with matching the bus width of the computer as they do with the speed of the RamSan chip. It is also more common to describe SIMM performance as 8 bit/16/32/64 bit. The following data is from a Kingston Memory webpage describing their ultimate guide to memory:

YEAR	MEMORY TYPE	ACCESS TIME
1987	FPM	50ns
1995	EDO	50ns
1997	SDRAM	15ns
1998	SDRAM	10ns
1999	SDRAM	7.5ns
2000	DDR SDRAM	3.75ns
2001	DDR SDRAM	3ns
2002	DDR SDRAM	2.3ns
2003	DDR SDRAM	2ns

The dramatic decrease in the cost of RAM is going to change Oracle database architectures. Since RAM was once a scarce and expensive resource, the Oracle DBA had to spend huge amounts of time managing Oracle memory allocation and optimization. Today 100 gigabytes of SSD (i.e. Texas Memory Systems) can be obtained for about $150,000. Less expensive solid state disks will mean a dramatic change in Oracle database architecture as the old-fashioned model of disk-based data management is abandoned in favor of a cache-based approach.

According to David Ensor, Oracle tuning expert, author and Former Vice President of the Oracle Corporation's Performance Group, the increase in CPU power has shifted the bottleneck of many systems to disk I/O.

> "Increased server power has meant that disk I/O has replaced CPU power and memory as the limiting factors on throughput for almost all applications and clustering is not a cost-effective way of increasing I/O throughput."

SSD as an Oracle Tuning Tool

The dramatic price:performance ratio of SSD is changing the way that Oracle databases are tuned. Sub-optimal Oracle databases no longer have to undergo expensive and time-consuming re-design. SSD technology is now competing head-on with Oracle consulting services.

For example, a poorly-designed Oracle database might take six-months and over $500,000 in consulting cost to repair. Using SSD as a remedy, the entire database will run more than ten times faster, within 24 hours, at a fraction of the cost of repairing the source code.

Fighting excessive disk I/O has always been a problem!

Of course, the code still runs sub-optimally, but the performance complaints are quickly alleviated at a very competitive cost.

SSD promises to radically change the way that Oracle databases are managed. Consequently, understanding the best approach to using this powerful new tool within Oracle architecture is essential.

Code Depot User ID = reader, Password = builder

RAM access speed with Oracle Databases

Now that inexpensive Sold-state disk is available, Oracle professionals are struggling to understand how to leverage this hardware for Oracle databases. Understanding the nature of Oracle RAM caching can help demonstrate the importance of this issue. The following sections will cover these topics:

- The history of Oracle RAM data buffering
- The problem of duplicitous RAM caches
- The issue of expensive logical I/O

A review of the existing research will provide insight into the best placement for SSD in an Oracle environment.

The History of Oracle RAM data buffering

When Oracle was first introduced in the early 1990's RAM was very expensive and very few databases could afford to run large data buffer regions. Because RAM was such a limited resource, Oracle utilized a least-frequently-used algorithm within the data buffer to ensure that only the most-frequently referenced data remained in the data buffer cache.

As of Oracle10g there are seven RAM data buffers to hold incoming data blocks. These RAM areas define RAM space for incoming data blocks and are governed by the following Oracle10g parameters. The sum of all of these parameter values determines the total space reserved for Oracle data blocks.

- *db_cache_size*
- *db_keep_cache_size*
- *db_recycle_cache_size*
- *db_2k_cache_size*
- *db_4k_cache_size*
- *db_8k_cache_size*
- *db_16k_cache_size*
- *db_32k_cache_size*

The following graphic plots the relationship between the size of the RAM data buffers and physical disk reads showing the non-linear nature of RAM scalability for Oracle (Figure 1.2).

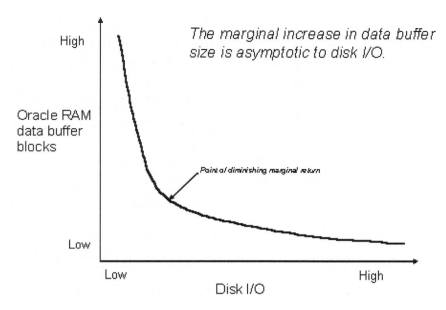

High

Oracle RAM
data buffer
blocks

The marginal increase in data buffer size is asymptotic to disk I/O.

Point of diminishing marginal return

Low

Low   High

Disk I/O

Figure 1.2 – *The relationship between physical disk I/O and the size of the RAM buffer cache*

This relationship can be expressed mathematically as:

$$\text{RAM Buffer Size} = \frac{n}{\text{Physical reads}}.$$

Where n = an observed constant

This relationship is the basis of the Automatic Memory Management (AMM) features of Oracle10g. Because the Automatic Workload Repository (AWR) is polling the efficiency of the data buffer, the AMM component can compute the point of diminishing marginal returns and re-assign SGA RAM resources to ensure optimal sizing for all seven Oracle10g data buffers.

Oracle uses this data to dynamically adjust each of the seven data buffers to keep them at their optimal size. AMM in Oracle 10g uses the AWR to collect historical buffer utilization information. The *dba_hist_db_cache_advice* view can be used to access this information for Oracle RAM management (Figure 1.3).

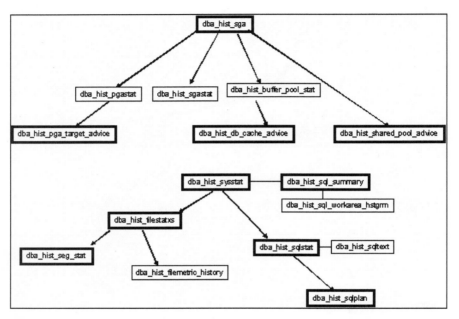

Figure 1.3 – *Oracle10g dba_hist views for Automated Memory Management (AMM)*

Additional RAM is very valuable when there is not enough RAM to cache the frequently-used data blocks. The diagram below demonstrates how a small increase in RAM results in a large decrease in disk I/O (Figure 1.4).

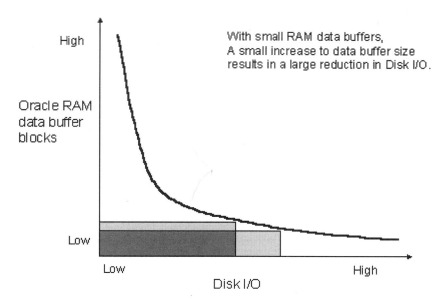

Figure 1.4 – *Too-small data buffers show large reduction of disk I/O*

Traditionally, the optimal size of the Oracle RAM data buffer cache has been the point where the marginal benefit begins to decline, as measured by the acceleration of the curve denoted in Figure 1.2.

However, this marginal benefit does not last forever. As full-caching of the Oracle database is approached, a relatively large amount of RAM is required to reduce physical disk I/O (Figure 1.5). This occurs because rarely read data blocks are now being pulled into the SGA data buffers.

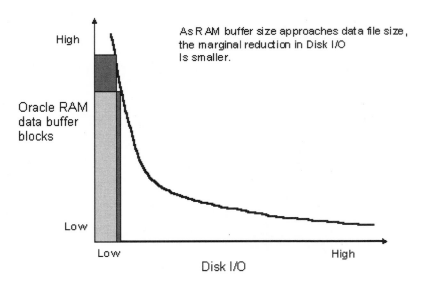

High

Oracle RAM
data buffer
blocks

Low

As RAM buffer size approaches data file size,
the marginal reduction in Disk I/O
Is smaller.

Low   High

Disk I/O

Figure 1.5 – *Diminishing value of RAM buffering as full-caching is approached*

This optimal point is calculated using the Oracle10g Automatic Memory Management (AMM) utility. To begin, take a look at the script to display the output from the Oracle *v$db_cache_advice* utility:

💾 **cache_advice.sql**

```
-- *************************************************
-- Copyright © 2003 by Rampant TechPress
-- This script is free for non-commercial purposes
-- with no warranties.  Use at your own risk.
--
-- To license this script for a commercial purpose,
-- contact info@rampant.cc
-- *************************************************

column c1    heading 'Cache Size (m)'          format 999,999,999,999
column c2    heading 'Buffers'                 format 999,999,999
column c3    heading 'Estd Phys|Read Factor'   format 999.90
column c4    heading 'Estd Phys| Reads'        format 999,999,999

select
   size_for_estimate              c1,
```

```
    buffers_for_estimate         c2,
    estd_physical_read_factor    c3,
    estd_physical_reads          c4
from
    v$db_cache_advice
where
    name = 'DEFAULT'
and
    block_size   = (SELECT value FROM V$PARAMETER
                    WHERE name = 'db_block_size')
And
    advice_status = 'ON';
```

When this utility is executed, the relationship between the RAM
buffer size and physical reads is demonstrated. Note that the
values range from 10 percent of the current size to double the
current size of the *db_cache_size*.

Cache Size (MB)	Buffers	Estd Phys Read Factor	Estd Phys Reads	
30	3,802	18.70	192,317,943	← 10% size
60	7,604	12.83	131,949,536	
91	11,406	7.38	75,865,861	
121	15,208	4.97	51,111,658	
152	19,010	3.64	37,460,786	
182	22,812	2.50	25,668,196	
212	26,614	1.74	17,850,847	
243	30,416	1.33	13,720,149	
273	34,218	1.13	11,583,180	
304	38,020	1.00	10,282,475	Current Size
334	41,822	.93	9,515,878	
364	45,624	.87	8,909,026	
395	49,426	.83	8,495,039	
424	53,228	.79	8,116,496	
456	57,030	.76	7,824,764	
486	60,832	.74	7,563,180	
517	64,634	.71	7,311,729	
547	68,436	.69	7,104,280	
577	72,238	.67	6,895,122	
608	76,040	.66	6,739,731	← 2x size

This predictive model is the basis for Oracle10g AMM. Figure
1.6 shows the tradeoff that occurs when data is taken from
Oracle's predictive mode and plotted.

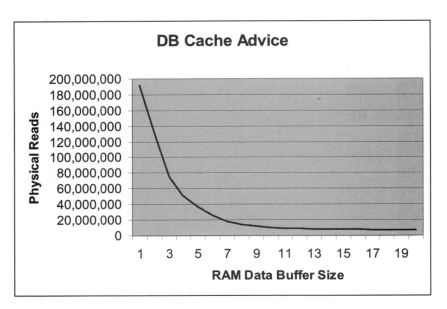

Figure 1.6 – *A plot from the output of v$db_cache_advice*

The main point of the relationship between RAM buffering and physical reads is that all Oracle databases have data that is accessed at different frequencies. In sum, the larger the number of frequently referenced data blocks, the greater the benefit from speeding-up block access.

The next step is to apply this knowledge to the use of SSD for Oracle.

Allocating Oracle Objects into Multiple RAM data Buffers

Since very few Oracle database can afford the cost of full RAM caching, many rules have developed for the segregation and isolation of cached objects. Some of these will provide clues about the best way to utilize SSD in a solid-state Oracle environment:

Segregate large-table full-table scans – Large tables that experience full-table scans will benefit from the largest supported block size and should be placed in a tablespace with the largest block size.

Use the RECYCLE Pool – The *db_recycle_cache_size* parameter should not be used if *db_cache_size* is not set to the largest supported block size for the server. Instead, create a *db_32k_cache_size* (or whatever the max is), and assign all large tables that experience frequent full-table scans to the largest buffer cache in the database.

Segregate Indexes - In many cases, Oracle SQL statements will retrieve index information via an index range scan, scanning the b-tree or bitmap index for ranges of values that match the SQL search criteria. Hence, it is beneficial to have as much of an index residing in RAM as possible. One of the very first things the Oracle 9i database administrator should do is migrate all Oracle indexes into a large blocksize tablespace. Indexes will always favor the largest supported blocksize.

Segregate random access reads - For those databases that fetch small rows randomly from the disk, the Oracle DBA can segregate these types of tables into 2K tablespaces. Even though disk space is becoming cheaper every day, try not to waste available RAM by reading in more information than is actually going to be used by the query. Hence, many Oracle DBAs will use small block sizes in situations of tiny, random access record retrieval.

Segregate LOB column tables - For those Oracle tables that contain raw, long raw, or in-line large objects (LOB), moving the table rows to large block sizes will have an extremely beneficial effect on disk I/O. Experienced DBAs will check *dba_tables.avg_row_len* to make sure that the blocksize is larger than the average size. Row chaining will be reduced while the entire LOB can be read within a single disk I/O, thereby avoiding the additional overhead of having Oracle read multiple blocks.

Segregate large-table full-table scan rows - When the recycle pool was first introduced in Oracle8i, the idea was to quickly flush the full table scan data blocks which are not likely to be re-read by other transactions through the Oracle SGA. The result is reserving critical RAM for those data blocks which are likely to be re-read by another transaction.

Check the average row length - The block size for a tables' tablespace should always be greater than the average row length for the table (*dba_tables.avg_row_len*). If it is smaller than the average row length, rows chaining occurs and excessive disk I/O is incurred.

Use large blocks for data sorting – The TEMP tablespace will benefit from the largest supported blocksize. This allows disk sorting to happen in large blocks with a minimum of disk I/O.

These suggestions are very important to the study of the best way to utilize SSD as an alternative caching mechanism.

However, recent TPC-C benchmarks make it clear that very-large RAM regions are a central component in high-performance Oracle databases. The 2004 UNISYS Oracle Windows benchmark exceeded 250,000 transactions per minute using a Windows-based 16-CPU server with 115 gigabytes of Oracle data buffer cache. Here are the Oracle parameters that were used in the benchmark. The benefit of large-scale RAM caching is clearly shown:

```
db_16k_cache_size   = 15010M
db_8k_cache_size    = 1024M
db_cache_size       = 8096M
db_keep_cache_size  = 78000M
```

At this point it is very clear that RAM resources are a very important factor in maintaining the performance of I/O intensive Oracle systems.

Monitoring Oracle can be very time-consuming.

Improving I/O speed is not a silver bullet

Please understand that SSD and RAM buffer caching are only important to I/O-intensive Oracle databases. If an Oracle database is constrained by other environmental factors such as the CPU or the network then speeding-up the I/O sub-system will not result in any appreciable performance gains. To learn more about database resource bottlenecks, display the top-5 timed events from STATSPACK.

Here is a typical OLTP database where I/O delay is the main source of wait time. Note that I/O comprises more than 70% of total elapsed time.

```
Top 5 Timed Events
~~~~~~~~~~~~~~~~~~                                       % Total
Event                          Waits       Time (s)     Ela Time
------------------------     ------------  -----------  --------
db file sequential read         2,598         7,146        48.54
db file scattered read         25,519         3,246        22.04
library cache load lock           673         1,363         9.26
CPU time                        1,154          7.83         6.21
log file parallel write        19,157           837         5.68
```

Again, it is critical to note that additional RAM resources may not have any appreciable effect on databases that are not I/O intensive. For example, some scientific Oracle databases only read a small set of experimental results and spend the majority of database time performing computations as evidenced by the report shown below.

```
Top 5 Timed Events
~~~~~~~~~~~~~~~~~~                                       % Total
Event                          Waits     Time (s)  Ela Time
------------------------     ------------  -----------  --------
CPU time                        4,851       4,042      55.76
db file sequential read         1,968       1,997      27.55
log file sync                 299,097         369       5.08
db file scattered read         53,031         330       4.55
log file parallel write       302,680         190       2.62
```

In this example, notice that CPU time is the primary source of database delay so improving the speed of the I/O with SSD may not have an appreciable effect on overall Oracle performance.

Be careful not to focus solely on minimizing physical disk I/O. For databases with sub-optimal SQL statements it is not uncommon to see poor performance combined with a very high data buffer cache hit ratio and very little disk I/O. For these databases, the root cause of the performance problem is excessive logical I/O, whereby the sub-optimal SQL re-reads data blocks over-and-over from the RAM data buffers.

Here are several myths of Oracle physical I/O:

All Oracle databases are I/O-bound – Untrue. Databases with a reasonable data buffer cache size and a small working set will usually be constrained by CPU or network latency.

The Data Buffer Hit Ratio will show caching efficiency – Untrue, except in cases of a super-small cache. The Data Buffer Hit ratio only measures the propensity that a data block will be in the buffer on the second I/O request.

Only faster disks can remove I/O bottlenecks – This is a common myth. There are other non-RAM approaches to reducing disk I/O for Oracle databases:

Adjusting *optimizer_mode* – Oracle will generate widely-differing SQL execution plans depending on the optimizer mode.

Re-analyze SQL optimizer statistics – Using better-quality CBO statistics with *dbms_stats* and adding column histograms can make a huge difference in disk activity.

Adjusting Oracle parameters – Re-setting the *optimizer_index_cost_adj* and *optimizer_index_caching* parameters can affect physical reads

Improve *clustering_factor* for index range scans - Manually re-sequence table rows to improve *clustering_factor,* sometimes using single-table clusters, can reduce disk I/O.

Use Materialized Views – Systems with batch-only updates may greatly benefit from Materialized Views to pre-join tables. Of course, the overhead of "refresh commit" is too great for high-update systems.

The next issue to be covered is duplicated RAM caching in large Oracle systems.

The problem of duplicitous RAM caches

As hardware evolved though the 1990's, independent components of database systems started to employ their own RAM caching tools (Figure 1-7).

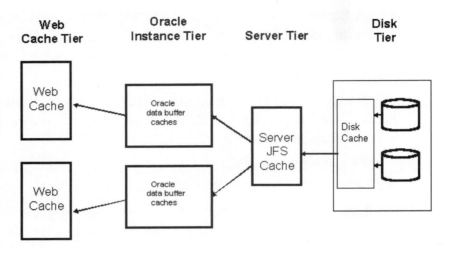

Figure 1-7 – *Multiple RAM caches in an Oracle enterprise*

As this figure demonstrates, the Oracle database is not the only component to utilize RAM caching. The disk array employs a RAM cache, the servers have a Journal File System (JFS) RAM cache, and the front-end web server also serves to cache Oracle data.

Working with older technology can be very difficult

This concept is important because many enterprises may inadvertently double-cache Oracle data. Even more problematic is the "fake" statistics reported by Oracle when multiple-level caches are employed:

Fake physical I/O times – If a disk array with a built-in RAM cache is being used, the disk I/O subsystem may acknowledge a physical write to the database even though the data has not yet been written to the physical disk spindle. This can skew timing of disk read/write speed.

Wasted Oracle Data Buffer RAM – In systems that employ web servers such as Apache, the front-end may cache frequently-used data. Consequently, Oracle resources may be wasted by

---

RAM access speed with Oracle Databases

caching data blocks that are already cached on the web server tier.

Now it is time to take a look at the best way to use SSD in an Oracle environment. Examining the relationship between Physical Disk I/O (PIO) and Oracle Logical I/O (LIO) is a good place to start.

Why is Oracle logical I/O so slow?

Disk latency is generally measured in milliseconds while RAM access is expressed in nanoseconds. In theory, RAM is four orders of magnitude or 10,000 times faster than disk. However, this is not true when using Oracle. In practice, logical I/O is seldom more than 1,000 times faster than disk I/O. Most Oracle experts say that logical disk I/O is only 15 to 100 times faster than physical disk I/O.

Oracle has internal data protection mechanisms at work that cause RAM data block access to be far slower due to internal locks and latch serialization mechanisms. This overhead is required by Oracle to maintain read consistency and data concurrency. So, if Oracle logical I/O is expensive, can this expense be avoided when data is read directly from disk? The answer can be found in determining the most appropriate placement for SSD in an Oracle environment.

With 144 gigabyte super-large disks becoming commonplace, I/O intensive databases will often see disk latency because many tasks are competing to read blocks on different parts of the super-large disk. An Oracle physical read must first read the disk data block and then transfer it into the Oracle RAM buffer before the data is passed to the requesting program (Figure 1-8).

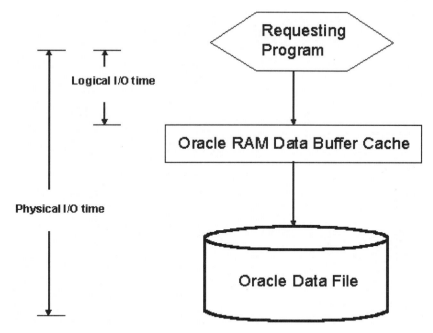

Figure 1-8 – *Physical reads include logical I/O latency*

Since logical I/O expense is going to happen regardless of whether or not physical I/O is performed, there is valuable insight to be gained into the proper placement for SSD in an Oracle environment:

Finding the Baselines

It is critical to remember that Oracle databases are always changing. A database examined at 10:00 AM may be completely different from the same database examined at 3:00 PM. When the performance of Oracle disk I/O is examined over time, signatures appear when the I/O information is aggregated by hours-of-the-day and day-of-the-week (Figure 1-9).

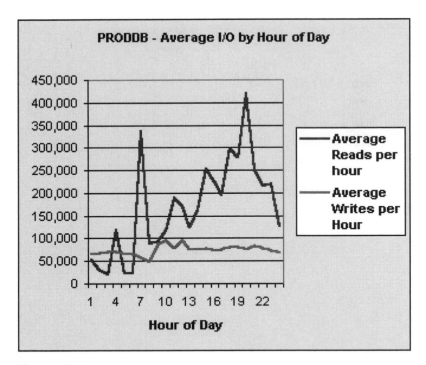

Figure 1-9 – *Average disk reads and writes by hour of the day*

Most Oracle professionals will use Oracle9i STATSPACK or Oracle10g AWR information to gather these baselines. Once the repeating I/O trends have been identified, a broad-brush approach to the application of SSD can be used. Thus, placing the fast I/O devices where they will do the most good.

Capturing I/O information at the file level can provide insight into the best data files to place on super-fast SSD. The *reads.sql* script extracts the physical read information from the Oracle 10g *dba_hist_filestatxs* view:

```
-- *************************************************
-- Copyright © 2003 by Rampant TechPress
-- This script is free for non-commercial purposes
-- with no warranties.  Use at your own risk.
--
-- To license this script for a commercial purpose,
-- contact info@rampant.cc
-- *************************************************

break on begin_interval_time skip 2

column phyrds  format 999,999,999
column begin_interval_time format a25

select
   begin_interval_time,
   filename,
   phyrds
from
   dba_hist_filestatxs
  natural join
   dba_hist_snapshot
;
```

The example that follows shows a running total of physical reads by datafile. Note that the snapshots are collected every half-hour. Starting from this script, a *where* clause criteria could easily be added to create a unique time-series exception report.

```
SQL> @reads

BEGIN_INTERVAL_TIME        FILENAME                                   PHYRDS
-------------------------   ----------------------------------------  -------
24-FEB-04 11.00.32.000 PM  E:\ORACLE\ORA92\FSDEV10G\SYSTEM01.DBF     164,700
                           E:\ORACLE\ORA92\FSDEV10G\UNDOTBS01.DBF     26,082
                           E:\ORACLE\ORA92\FSDEV10G\SYSAUX01.DBF     472,008
                           E:\ORACLE\ORA92\FSDEV10G\USERS01.DBF        1,794
                           E:\ORACLE\ORA92\FSDEV10G\T_FS_LSQ.ORA       2,123

24-FEB-04 11.30.18.296 PM  E:\ORACLE\ORA92\FSDEV10G\SYSTEM01.DBF     167,809
                           E:\ORACLE\ORA92\FSDEV10G\UNDOTBS01.DBF     26,248
                           E:\ORACLE\ORA92\FSDEV10G\SYSAUX01.DBF     476,616
                           E:\ORACLE\ORA92\FSDEV10G\USERS01.DBF        1,795
                           E:\ORACLE\ORA92\FSDEV10G\T_FS_LSQ.ORA       2,244

25-FEB-04 12.01.06.562 AM  E:\ORACLE\ORA92\FSDEV10G\SYSTEM01.DBF     169,940
                           E:\ORACLE\ORA92\FSDEV10G\UNDOTBS01.DBF     26,946
                           E:\ORACLE\ORA92\FSDEV10G\SYSAUX01.DBF     483,550
                           E:\ORACLE\ORA92\FSDEV10G\USERS01.DBF        1,799
                           E:\ORACLE\ORA92\FSDEV10G\T_FS_LSQ.ORA       2,248
```

Of course, with a little tweaking to the *reads.sql* script, reports on physical writes, read time, write time, single block reads, and a host of other neat metrics from the *dba_hist_filestatxs* view could be generated.

Next the existing research on SSD will be reviewed and supplemented by what other Oracle experts say about using SSD with Oracle.

A Review of existing SSD Research findings

Different researchers are coming to different conclusions about the applicability of SSD to Oracle systems. There are three research papers on SSD and each arrive at similar conclusions about the use of SSD with Oracle. Complete references are included in the References section at the end of this section. Here is a summary of the findings from each study.

Some top Oracle experts have examined SSD technology

James Morle

According to (Morle, 2002), SSD is great for Oracle redo logs, undo tablespace (rollback segment tablespace in Oracle8i), and the TEMP tablespace. He notes that for rollback segments, SSD is a great help:

> "This is where SSD can help out. By deploying a single SSD, all redo logs can be located away from the RAID 1+0 array, whilst providing low latency writes and high bandwidth reads (for archiving)."

Morle also asserts that full-caching of a database on SSD may not improve performance:

> "If the whole database were running from SSD, there would be enormous pieces of unnecessary work going on, such as:
>
> Management of the buffer cache
>
> Context switches into kernel mode to perform I/O
>
> Conversion of the request into SCSI/Fibre Channel
>
> Transmission across the SAN
>
> And all the way back again
>
> In comparison to disk I/O, this whole process is stunningly fast. In comparison to just reading the data straight from user space memory, however, it is incredibly slow!"

Morle notes that a typical OLTP system maintains a working set of frequently referenced data blocks, and those might be good candidates for SSD. For DSS and Data Warehouse systems, Morle advocates moving the current table partitions onto SSD devices, leaving the others on traditional disk.

Dr. Paul Dorsey

In another landmark SSD study in 2004, Dr, Paul Dorsey showed that the SSD data transfer rates are always better than traditional disk:

Device	Test#1: Buffered Read	Test #2: Sequential Read	Test #3: Random Read	Test #4: Buffered Write	Test #5: Sequential Write	Test #6: Random Write
RamSan	95	98	98	86	84	82
IDE	85	40	6	65	38	11
SCSI	65	33	9	49	33	11

Dr. Dorsey concludes:

"Technologically, SSD is one of the best sources of performance improvement for an Oracle database if you have a typical OLTP system including many transactions which access different small amounts of random data and lots of users.

SSDs may also improve data warehouse applications because of the improved query performance. There is no generic answer for all questions, but solid state disks represent another way of thinking about managing enterprise-wide databases."

Woody Hutsell

In his Texas Memory Systems whitepaper titled *Faster Oracle Database Access with the RAMSAN-210* (2001), Hutsell concludes that certain types of Oracle databases will always benefit from SSD:

There are some databases that should have all of their files moved to solid state disk. These databases tend to have at least one of the following characteristics:

High concurrent access. Databases that are being hit by a large number of concurrent users should consider storing all of their data on solid state disk. This will make sure that storage is not a bottleneck for the application and maximize the utilization of servers and networks. I/O wait time will be minimized and servers and bandwidth will be fully utilized.

Frequent random accesses to all tables. For some databases, it is impossible to identify a subset of files that are frequently accessed. Many times these databases are effectively large indices.

Small to medium size databases. Given the fixed costs associated with buying RAID systems, it is often economical to buy a solid state disk to store small to medium sized databases. A RamSan-210, for example, can provide 32GB of database storage for the price of some enterprise RAID systems.

SSD Conclusions

Research indicates that SSD can be very valuable to Oracle databases, with the total benefit depending on the type of processing characteristics.

Use SSD for high-impact files – Oracle redo log files, undo segment, and temporary tablespace file will greatly benefit from SSD.

SSD has impressive speed improvements - (Dorsey, 2004) reported a 67% gain (.67x) in data access speed with SSD. (Morle, 2002) noted a reported a 25% (.25x) increase in system speed with SSD

SSD may shift the Oracle bottleneck to CPU – SSD should only be attempted when CPU consumption (as measured by a STATSPACK top-5 wait event report) is less than 50% of the consumption. Using SSD will shift the bottleneck from I/O

---

to CPU, and the server may require more CPU's to improve dispatching, or faster CPU's (e.g. Itanium2 processors).

Read-intensive system benefit most from SSD – Write-intensive systems, especially those with high buffer invalidations, may only see a marginal speed improvement.

SSD will speed-up access on super-large disks – The 114 gigabyte disk often experiences disk enqueues as competing tasks wait their turn at the read-write heads. SSD will surely improve throughput for these types of database disks.

References:

Dorsey, P, Solid State Disks: Sorting out the Myths from the Reality, IOUG SELECT Magazine (2004)

Morle, J, Solid State Disks in an Oracle Environment: The New Rules of Deployment, Scale Abilities Ltd., 2002.

Hutsell, W, Faster Oracle Database Access with the RAMSAN-210, Texas Memory Systems,
http://www.storagesearch.com/texasmemsysart1.pdf

SSD Benchmark Hypothesis

Now that the issues surrounding SSD in an Oracle environment have been covered, it is time to hypothesize about the results of the benchmark tests.

In reviewing the existing research and applying logic to the results, large performance gains can be realized by placing specific types of databases on SSD. Specifically databases that are predominantly read based, such as decision support (DSS) or data warehouse, should benefit the most. In order to determine if this is indeed the case, use the TPCH benchmark, which is designed for DSS testing.

Time to develop an SSD test plan

The central issue of this study is to determine the benefit of SSD for Oracle under these conditions:

No SSD with a super-large Oracle data buffer – This can minimize PIO with only one physical read into the data buffer, but cause LIO overhead.

SSD with a tiny Oracle data buffer – This makes PIO faster, but will cause repeated LIO overhead as data blocks are aged-out of the Oracle data buffer. It is expected that LIO overhead would be huge with high latch contention, buffer busy waits, and free buffer waits.

SSD for files with large Oracle Data buffer cache – This is duplicating RAM but it would relieve the LIO issue.

Assuming that SSD is far faster for PIO, the issue of duplicitous Oracle activity still remains. At PIO time, the data block must still be read into *db_cache_size* and then a consistent get is required to deliver the data block to the requesting program. Hence, RAM resources appear to be better allocated directly to *db_cache_size* instead of using the RAM with SSD.

Specific architectures

Large data buffers with SSD for:

- Redo log files
- Undo segments
- Temporary tablespace blocks

Predictions

If it is assumed that SSD is far faster for PIO, the issue of duplicitous Oracle activity still remains. At PIO time, the data block must still be read into *db_cache_size* and then a consistent get is required to deliver the data block to the requesting program. Hence, RAM resources appear to be better allocated directly to *db_cache_size* instead of using RAM with SSD.

The benchmark study that was created specifically to test these hypotheses and show conclusively how Oracle functions with solid-state disk will follow in the next Chapter.

Conclusion

In this chapter, the importance of the SSD array for its current and potential values was covered. It is predicted that within the next decade, through such advances as quantum state memory, the size and cost of memory will soon drop to less than disk costs. When this happens, the IT industry will likely abandon the spinning rust concept of memory storage and move to SSD technology.

This book is designed to assist in preparation for that day when SSD technology is as plentiful and cheap as disk. DBAs will need to make the logical choice of how and when to use SSD technology.

In the next few chapters, the testing methodologies, tests and conclusions from testing SSD technology for use with Oracle databases will be covered.

Choosing a Benchmark   CHAPTER

2

In deciding to perform a series of tests to evaluate the effectiveness of using solid-state disk drives with the Oracle database system, a test bed that showcased state-of-the-art technology had to be obtained. Texas Memory Systems provided access and sole use to a 64 gigabyte TMS solid state drive, a set of Linux servers and a 64 gigabyte SCSI (and later SATA) disk array. Over the period of May through August of 2004 a series of tests was conducted utilizing version 9.2.0.4 of the Oracle database system and various configurations of the SSD, server and SCSI/SATA drives to evaluate the effectiveness of various combinations.

In reviewing the existing research and applying logic to the results a large performance gain should be seen from placing entire specific types of databases on SSD. Specifically databases that are predominantly read-based such as decision support (DSS) or data warehouses should benefit the most. In order to determine if this is indeed a fact, the TPCH benchmark will be used. The TPCH benchmark was designed for DSS testing

The next section will provide an overview of the details behind the TPCH benchmark in order to demonstrate the reasoning for this choice.

TPC Benchmark H Overview

The TPC Benchmark™ H (TPC-H) is a decision support benchmark. It consists of a suite of business oriented ad-hoc queries and concurrent data modifications. The queries and the data populating the database have been chosen to have broad industry-wide relevance while maintaining a sufficient degree of ease of implementation. This benchmark illustrates decision support systems that:

- Examine large volumes of data;
- Execute queries with a high degree of complexity;
- Give answers to critical business questions.

Choose a benchmark that matches typical processing!

TPC-H evaluates the performance of various decision support systems by the execution of sets of queries against a standard database under controlled conditions. The TPC-H queries:

- Give answers to real-world business questions;
- Simulate generated ad-hoc queries via a point and click GUI interface;
- Are far more complex than most OLTP transactions;

- Include a rich breadth of operators and selectivity constraints;

- Generate intensive activity on the part of the database server component of the system under test;

- Are executed against a database complying with specific population and scaling requirements;

- Are implemented with constraints derived from staying closely synchronized with an on-line production database.

The TPC-H operations are modeled as follows:

- The database is continuously available 24 hours a day, 7 days a week, for ad-hoc queries from multiple end users and updates against all tables, except possibly during infrequent (e.g., once a month) maintenance sessions.

- The TPC-H database tracks, possibly with some delay, the state of the OLTP database through ongoing updates which batch together a number of modifications impacting some part of the decision support database.

- Due to the world-wide nature of the business data stored in the TPC-H database, the queries and the updates may be executed against the database at any time, especially in relation to each other. In addition, this mix of queries and updates is subject to specific ACIDity requirements, since queries and updates may execute concurrently;

- To achieve the optimal compromise between performance and operational requirements the database administrator can set, once and for all, the locking levels and the concurrent scheduling rules for queries and updates.

- The minimum database required to run the benchmark holds business data from 10,000 suppliers. It contains almost ten million rows representing a raw storage capacity of about 1 GB. Compliant benchmark implementations may also use one of the larger permissible database populations (e.g. 1,000 GB). The TPC believes that comparisons of TPC-H results measured against different database sizes are misleading and discourages such comparisons. For this TMS benchmark a 20 gigabyte implementation of the standard TPC-H benchmark database generated by the *dbgen* program will be used.

- The TPC-H database must be implemented using a commercially available database management system (DBMS), and the queries executed via an interface using dynamic SQL. The specification provides for variants of SQL, as implementers are not required to have implemented a specific SQL standard in full. TPC-D uses terminology and metrics that are similar to other benchmarks, originated by the TPC and others. Such similarity in terminology does not in any way imply that TPC-H results are comparable to other benchmarks. The only benchmark results comparable to TPC-H are other TPC-H results compliant with the same revision.

Despite the fact that this benchmark offers a rich environment representative of many decision support systems, this benchmark does not reflect the entire range of decision support requirements. In addition, the extent to which a customer can achieve the results reported by a vendor is highly dependent on how closely TPC-H approximates the customer application. The relative performance of systems derived from this benchmark does not necessarily hold for other workloads or environments. Extrapolations to any other environment are not recommended.

Management should insist on representative benchmarks

Benchmark results are highly dependent upon workload, specific application requirements, and systems design and implementation. Relative system performance will vary as a result of these and other factors. Therefore, TPC-H should not be used as a substitute for a specific customer application benchmarking when critical capacity planning and/or product evaluation decisions are contemplated.

When doing a benchmark it's important to choose appropriate hardware

Now, the next topic to cover is the selection of hardware for an SSD benchmark.

Benchmark Hardware Architecture

SSD technology is available for use with most operating systems and architectures. The SSD from Texas Memory Systems for example is treated as a standard SCSI Fiber attached disk array.

In picking the architecture for this series of tests it was decided to use the Intel based commodity type architecture which is one of the fastest growing architectures today. This would allow the tests to be recreated by anyone with even a modest equipment budget.

The server architecture used in the study consisted of the following hardware:

2-Linux Servers each with:

- 2 - 1.88 GHz AMD 244 CPUs each with .75MB I-cache, 1.5MB D-cache.
- 4 GB PC2700 DDR-33 Memory
- 1 PCI Fibre Channel 2X Card
- 1 PCI Lan Adapter
- 1 DVD ROM
- 2 SCSI Cards

In choosing the disk architecture it was felt that using SCSI would best show the same level of hardware utilized by a majority of sites. However, the failure of the SCSI array early in the testing forced the switch to an ATA disk array that was ultimately the architecture used. Therefore a disk array subsystem consisting of the following was used:

- 1 SCSI Array (with a total of 2 - 36GB 10000 RPM Disks)
- 1 ATA array (with a total of 7-200GB 7200 RPM Disks)
- 1 Texas Memory System 64 Gigabyte SSD Array

The system used in the study is diagramed in Figure 2.1.

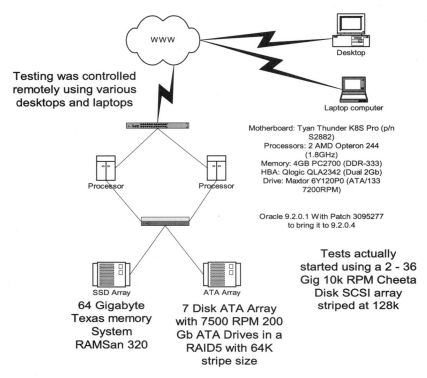

Figure 2.1: *Testing Architecture*

Once the basic test plan (TPCH) and test architecture were chosen the exact methodology to be utilized had to be decided.

Benchmark Methodology

In many benchmark tests multiple "tricks" are used to obtain the desired results, for example some tests use undocumented Oracle parameters to force Oracle into a "federated" architecture during RAC tests. Others use excessive memory settings or require hardware that would never be utilized in a true operating situation. The purpose of these tests is not to skew the results in favor of a desired outcome, but to represent the SSD architecture as it would be applied in a standard environment. Therefore the desired methodology used during this test had to meet the following requirements:

- Be easily repeated by anyone desiring to do so

- Not involve complex, undocumented initialization parameters

- Utilize off-the-shelf components in a standard configuration

- Database size and configuration should be as "real-world" as possible

Determine a meaningful methodology first!

To meet these requirements it was decided to utilize the TPCH benchmark database and query generator. The *dbgen* and *qgen* programs are available as a download from the www.tpc.org website. In order to ensure the test was applicable to as wide an audience as possible the database size was set at 20 gigabytes, which for the TPCH benchmark translated into 54 gigabytes once indexes and support tablespaces are added.

The test method involved the following steps:

1. Download and compile the TPCH benchmark programs using standard options and C compiler. The selected compile options where for Solaris, SQL Server. Oracle was not a listed option, but SQL Server provided standard SQL statements.

2. Ftp'ed 20000511.tar.z, which was downloaded from www.ftp.org, to aultlinux1 and used gunzip and tar to extract files.

3. cd'ed to dbgen directory

4. Used cp to copy makefile.suite to makefile

5. Used vi to edit makefile to set variables:
   ```
   DATABASE = SQLSERVER (Oracle option not available)
   MACHINE=SUN (closest to LINUX, DOS didn't work)
   WORKLOAD = TPCH
   ```

6. Ran command "make"

7. Download and install latest Oracle 9i database and required patch (3095277) to bring the database to 9.2.0.4 on the internal disk drives for Linux server.

8. Download and install client software on second Linux box

9. Configure solid state drive and SCSI/ATA drives using standard Linux disk formatting and file systems commands using filesystem 2 no-journaling devices.

```
pvcreate -d /dev/sda
pvcreate -d /dev/sdb
vgcreate -l 256 -p 256 -s 128k /dev/dss_volume /dev/sda
vgcreate -l 256 -p 256 -s 128k /dev/dss_volume2 /dev/sdb
lvcreate -L 10g /dev/dss_volume /dev/dss_vol11
lvcreate -L 10g /dev/dss_volume /dev/dss_vol12
lvcreate -L 10g /dev/dss_volume /dev/dss_vol13
lvcreate -L 8g /dev/dss_volume /dev/dss_vol14
lvcreate -L 8g /dev/dss_volume /dev/dss_vol15
lvcreate -L 8g /dev/dss_volume /dev/dss_vol16
lvcreate -L 8g /dev/dss_volume /dev/dss_vol17
lvcreate -L 10g /dev/dss_volume2 /dev/dss_vol21
lvcreate -L 10g /dev/dss_volume2 /dev/dss_vol22
lvcreate -L 10g /dev/dss_volume2 /dev/dss_vol23
lvcreate -L 8g /dev/dss_volume2 /dev/dss_vol24
lvcreate -L 8g /dev/dss_volume2 /dev/dss_vol25
lvcreate -L 8g /dev/dss_volume2 /dev/dss_vol26
lvcreate -L 8g /dev/dss_volume2 /dev/dss_vol27
e2mkfs /dev/dss_vol11 through /dev/dss_vol27
mkdir /u01 through /u14
chown oracle.dba /u01 through /u14
mount /dev/dss_vol11 /u01 through /dev/dss_vol27 /u14
```

10. In order to create the database, the *dbca* utility provided by Oracle was utilized to generate a standard set of scripts for a DSS database excluding the example schemas.

🖫 Createdb.sql

```
-- ***************************************************
-- Copyright © 2003 by Rampant TechPress
-- This script is free for non-commercial purposes
-- with no warranties.  Use at your own risk.
--
-- To license this script for a commercial purpose,
-- contact info@rampant.cc
-- ***************************************************

connect / as SYSDBA
set echo on
spool /home/oracle/assistants/dbca/logs/CreateDB.log
startup nomount pfile="/home/oracle/admin/dss/scripts/init.ora";
CREATE DATABASE dss
 MAXINSTANCES 2
 MAXLOGHISTORY 1
 MAXLOGFILES 5
 MAXLOGMEMBERS 3
 MAXDATAFILES 100
DATAFILE '/u01/oracle/oradata/dss/system01.dbf' SIZE 250M
 REUSE AUTOEXTEND ON NEXT  10240K MAXSIZE UNLIMITED
 EXTENT MANAGEMENT LOCAL
DEFAULT TEMPORARY TABLESPACE TEMP
 TEMPFILE '/u05/oracle/oradata/dss/temp01.dbf' SIZE 400M REUSE
 AUTOEXTEND ON NEXT  640K MAXSIZE UNLIMITED
```

```
UNDO TABLESPACE "UNDOTBS1"
 DATAFILE '/u04/oracle/oradata/dss/undotbs01.dbf' SIZE 200M REUSE
 AUTOEXTEND ON NEXT  5120K MAXSIZE UNLIMITED
CHARACTER SET WE8MSWIN1252
NATIONAL CHARACTER SET AL16UTF16
LOGFILE
 GROUP 1 ('/u02/oracle/oradata/dss/redo01.log') SIZE 102400K,
 GROUP 2 ('/u03/oracle/oradata/dss/redo02.log') SIZE 102400K,
 GROUP 3 ('/u02/oracle/oradata/dss/redo03.log') SIZE 102400K;
spool off
exit;


createdbfiles.sql

connect / as SYSDBA
set echo on
spool /home/oracle/ora9i/assistants/dbca/logs/CreateDBFiles.log

CREATE TABLESPACE "DRSYS" LOGGING DATAFILE
'/u02/oracle/oradata/dss/drsys01.dbf' SIZE 20M REUSE AUTOEXTEND ON
NEXT  640K
MAXSIZE UNLIMITED EXTENT MANAGEMENT LOCAL SEGMENT SPACE MANAGEMENT
AUTO ;

CREATE TABLESPACE "TOOLS" LOGGING DATAFILE
'/u02/oracle/oradata/dss/tools01.dbf' SIZE 50m REUSE AUTOEXTEND ON
NEXT  128K
MAXSIZE 8192m EXTENT MANAGEMENT LOCAL SEGMENT SPACE MANAGEMENT
AUTO ;

CREATE TABLESPACE "XDB" LOGGING DATAFILE
'/u03/oracle/oradata/dss/xdb01.dbf' SIZE 20M REUSE AUTOEXTEND ON
NEXT  640K
MAXSIZE UNLIMITED EXTENT MANAGEMENT LOCAL SEGMENT SPACE MANAGEMENT
AUTO ;
spool off
exit;


createDBCatalog.sql

connect / as SYSDBA
set echo on

spool /home/oracle/assistants/dbca/logs/CreateDBCatalog.log
@/home/oracle/rdbms/admin/catalog.sql;
@/home/oracle/rdbms/admin/catexp7.sql;
@/home/oracle/rdbms/admin/catblock.sql;
@/home/oracle/rdbms/admin/catproc.sql;
@/home/oracle/rdbms/admin/catoctk.sql;
@/home/oracle/rdbms/admin/owminst.plb;
connect SYSTEM/manager
@/home/oracle/sqlplus/admin/pupbld.sql;
connect SYSTEM/manager
set echo on
spool /home/oracle/assistants/dbca/logs/sqlPlusHelp.log
@/home/oracle/sqlplus/admin/help/hlpbld.sql helpus.sql;
spool off
```

```
spool off
exit;

intermedia.sql

connect / as SYSDBA
set echo on
spool /home/oracle/assistants/dbca/logs/interMedia.log
@/home/oracle/ord/im/admin/iminst.sql;
spool off
exit;

context.sql

connect / as SYSDBA
set echo on
spool /home/oracle/assistants/dbca/logs/context.log
@/home/oracle/ctx/admin/dr0csys change_on_install DRSYS TEMP;
connect CTXSYS/change_on_install
@/home/oracle/ctx/admin/dr0inst /home/oracle/bin/oractxx9.dll;
@/home/oracle/ctx/admin/defaults/dr0defin.sql AMERICAN;
spool off
exit;

xdbprotocol.sql

connect / as SYSDBA
set echo on
spool /home/oracle/assistants/dbca/logs/xdb_protocol.log
@/home/oracle/rdbms/admin/catqm.sql change_on_install XDB TEMP;
connect / as SYSDBA
@/home/oracle/rdbms/admin/catxdbj.sql;
spool off
exit;

jserver.sql

connect / as SYSDBA
set echo on
spool /home/oracle/assistants/dbca/logs/JServer.log
@/home/oracle/javavm/install/initjvm.sql;
@/home/oracle/xdk/admin/initxml.sql;
@/home/oracle/xdk/admin/xmlja.sql;
@/home/oracle/rdbms/admin/catjava.sql;
spool off
exit;

connect / as SYSDBA
set echo on
spool /home/oracle/assistants/dbca/logs/postDBCreation.log
@/home/oracle/rdbms/admin/utlrp.sql;
shutdown ;
connect / as SYSDBA
set echo on
spool /home/oracle/ora9i/assistants/dbca/logs/postDBCreation.log
create spfile='/home/oracle/database/spfiledss.ora' FROM
pfile='/home/oracle/admin/dss/scripts/init.ora';
```

```
startup ;
exit;
```

11. Next, scripts were manually generated to create required the tablespaces to support the benchmark (*dss_data* and *dss_index*).

    This is the script for the DSS portion of the benchmark. The SCSI/ATA portion script was identical except for the substitution of the appropriate SCSI/ATA filesystem, for example, u08 for u01, u09 for u02, etc.

```
create tablespace dss_data datafile
'/u01/oracle/oradata/dss/dss_data01.dbf' size 9000m,
'/u02/oracle/oradata/dss/dss_data02.dbf' size 8000m,
'/u03/oracle/oradata/dss/dss_data03.dbf' size 8000m
extent management local segment space management auto
/
create tablespace dss_index datafile
'/u04/oracle/oradata/dss/dss_index01.dbf' size 8300m,
'/u06/oracle/oradata/dss/dss_index02.dbf' size 7500m,
'/u07/oracle/oradata/dss/dss_index03.dbf' size 7500m
extent management local segment space management auto
/
```

12. After the required DSS tablespaces are created the DSS_ADMIN user is created using the following manually generated script.

```
create user dss_admin identified by dss_admin
default tablespace dss_data
quota unlimited on dss_data
quota unlimited on dss_index;
grant resource, dba, connect to dss_admin
/
```

13. Once the tablespaces and user were in place the *dss_admin* schema was built based on the table descriptions given in the DSS benchmark documentation. A manual script was generated to create these tables.

⊟ Table generator

```
-- **************************************************
-- Copyright © 2003 by Rampant TechPress
-- This script is free for non-commercial purposes
-- with no warranties.  Use at your own risk.
--
-- To license this script for a commercial purpose,
-- contact info@rampant.cc
-- **************************************************

create table PART
(p_partkey number not null,
p_name varchar2(55),
p_mfgr char(25),
p_brand char(10),
p_type varchar2(25),
p_size integer,
p_container char(10),
p_retailprice decimal(12,2),
p_comment varchar2(23),
constraint part_pk primary key (p_partkey)
using index
tablespace dss_index) nologging;

create table REGION
(r_regionkey number not null,
r_name char(25),
r_comment varchar2(152),
constraint region_Pk primary key (r_regionkey)
using index
tablespace dss_index) nologging;

create table NATION
(n_nationkey number not null,
n_name char(25),
n_regionkey number not null,
n_comment varchar2(152),
constraint nation_pk primary key (n_nationkey)
using index
tablespace dss_index,
constraint nat_region_fk foreign key (n_regionkey)
references region(r_regionkey)) nologging;

create table SUPPLIER
(s_suppkey number not null,
s_name char(25),
s_address varchar2(40),
s_nationkey number not null,
s_phone char(15),
s_acctbal decimal(12,2),
s_comment varchar2(101),
constraint supplier_pk primary key (s_suppkey)
using index
tablespace dss_index,
```

```
constraint supp_nation_fk foreign key (s_nationkey)
references nation(n_nationkey)) nologging;

create table PARTSUPP
(ps_partkey number not null,
ps_suppkey number not null,
ps_availqty integer,
ps_supplycost decimal(12,2),
ps_comment varchar2(199),
constraint partsupp_pk primary key (ps_partkey, ps_suppkey)
using index
tablespace dss_index,
constraint partsupp_part foreign key (ps_partkey) references
part(p_partkey),
constraint partsupp_supp foreign key (ps_suppkey) references
supplier(s_suppkey)) nologging;

create table CUSTOMER
(c_custkey number not null,
c_name varchar2(25),
c_address varchar2(40),
c_nationkey number not null,
c_phone char(15),
c_acctbal decimal(12,2),
c_mktsegment char(10),
c_comment varchar2(117),
constraint customer_pk primary key (c_custkey)
using index
tablespace dss_index,
constraint cust_nation_fk foreign key (c_nationkey) references
nation(n_nationkey)) nologging;

create table ORDERS
(o_orderkey number not null,
o_custkey number not null,
o_orderstatus char,
o_totalprice decimal(12,2),
o_orderdate date,
o_orderpriority char(15),
o_clerk char(15),
o_shippriority integer,
o_comment varchar2(79),
constraint orders_pk primary key (o_orderkey)
using index
tablespace dss_index,
constraint order_cust_fk foreign key (o_orderkey) references
orders(o_orderkey)) nologging;

create table LINEITEM
(l_orderkey number not null,
l_partkey number not null,
l_suppkey number not null,
l_linenumber integer,
l_quantity decimal(12,2),
l_extendedprice decimal(12,2),
l_discount decimal(4,2),
l_tax number,
```

```
l_returnflag char,
l_linestatus char,
l_shipdate date,
l_commitdate date,
l_receiptdate date,
l_shipinstruct char(25),
l_shipmode char(10),
l_comment varchar2(44),
constraint lineitem_pk primary key (l_orderkey,l_linenumber)
using index
tablespace dss_index,
constraint linei_partsupp_fk foreign key (l_partkey,l_suppkey)
references partsupp(ps_partkey, ps_suppkey)) nologging;
```

14. Next, the flat files used to load the database were generated using the *dbgen* utility:

```
$ export DSS_PATH=/home/oracle/benchmark/tables
$ dbgen -s 20 -C 10
```

15. Once the database was ready and the required flat files generated, the Oracle supplied SQLLoader utility was used to load the database. Example parameter files used and example of loaded data are provided in Appendix A. The load process was scripted.

🖫 Load_data.sh

```
-- ****************************************************
-- Copyright © 2003 by Rampant TechPress
-- This script is free for non-commercial purposes
-- with no warranties.  Use at your own risk.
--
-- To license this script for a commercial purpose,
-- contact info@rampant.cc
-- ****************************************************

#!/bin/bash
set +x
date
sqlldr dss_admin/dss_admin control=part1.ctl log=part.log rows=1000
bindarraysize=1000000
sqlldr dss_admin/dss_admin control=part2.ctl log=part.log rows=1000
bindarraysize=1000000
sqlldr dss_admin/dss_admin control=part3.ctl log=part.log rows=1000
bindarraysize=1000000
sqlldr dss_admin/dss_admin control=part4.ctl log=part.log rows=1000
bindarraysize=1000000
sqlldr dss_admin/dss_admin control=part5.ctl log=part.log rows=1000
bindarraysize=1000000
sqlldr dss_admin/dss_admin control=part6.ctl log=part.log rows=1000
bindarraysize=1000000
```

```
sqlldr dss_admin/dss_admin control=part7.ctl log=part.log rows=1000
bindarraysize=1000000
sqlldr dss_admin/dss_admin control=part8.ctl log=part.log rows=1000
bindarraysize=1000000
sqlldr dss_admin/dss_admin control=part9.ctl log=part.log rows=1000
bindarraysize=1000000
sqlldr dss_admin/dss_admin control=part10.ctl log=part.log
rows=1000 bindarraysize=1000000

sqlldr dss_admin/dss_admin control=region.ctl log=region.log
rows=1000 bindarraysize=1000000
sqlldr dss_admin/dss_admin control=nation.ctl log=nation.log
rows=1000 bindarraysize=1000000
sqlldr dss_admin/dss_admin control=supplier1.ctl log=supplier.log
rows=1000 bindarraysize=1000000
sqlldr dss_admin/dss_admin control=supplier2.ctl log=supplier.log
rows=1000 bindarraysize=1000000
sqlldr dss_admin/dss_admin control=supplier3.ctl log=supplier.log
rows=1000 bindarraysize=1000000
sqlldr dss_admin/dss_admin control=supplier4.ctl log=supplier.log
rows=1000 bindarraysize=1000000
sqlldr dss_admin/dss_admin control=supplier5.ctl log=supplier.log
rows=1000 bindarraysize=1000000
sqlldr dss_admin/dss_admin control=supplier6.ctl log=supplier.log
rows=1000 bindarraysize=1000000
sqlldr dss_admin/dss_admin control=supplier7.ctl log=supplier.log
rows=1000 bindarraysize=1000000
sqlldr dss_admin/dss_admin control=supplier8.ctl log=supplier.log
rows=1000 bindarraysize=1000000
sqlldr dss_admin/dss_admin control=supplier9.ctl log=supplier.log
rows=1000 bindarraysize=1000000
sqlldr dss_admin/dss_admin control=supplier10.ctl log=supplier.log
rows=1000 bindarraysize=1000000

sqlldr dss_admin/dss_admin control=partsupp1.ctl log=partsupp.log
rows=1000 bindarraysize=1000000
sqlldr dss_admin/dss_admin control=partsupp2.ctl log=partsupp.log
rows=1000 bindarraysize=1000000
sqlldr dss_admin/dss_admin control=partsupp3.ctl log=partsupp.log
rows=1000 bindarraysize=1000000
sqlldr dss_admin/dss_admin control=partsupp4.ctl log=partsupp.log
rows=1000 bindarraysize=1000000
sqlldr dss_admin/dss_admin control=partsupp5.ctl log=partsupp.log
rows=1000 bindarraysize=1000000
sqlldr dss_admin/dss_admin control=partsupp6.ctl log=partsupp.log
rows=1000 bindarraysize=1000000
sqlldr dss_admin/dss_admin control=partsupp7.ctl log=partsupp.log
rows=1000 bindarraysize=1000000
sqlldr dss_admin/dss_admin control=partsupp8.ctl log=partsupp.log
rows=1000 bindarraysize=1000000
sqlldr dss_admin/dss_admin control=partsupp9.ctl log=partsupp.log
rows=1000 bindarraysize=1000000
sqlldr dss_admin/dss_admin control=partsupp10.ctl log=partsupp.log
rows=1000 bindarraysize=1000000

sqlldr dss_admin/dss_admin control=customer1.ctl log=customer.log
rows=1000 bindarraysize=1000000
```

```
sqlldr dss_admin/dss_admin control=customer2.ctl log=customer.log
rows=1000 bindarraysize=1000000
sqlldr dss_admin/dss_admin control=customer3.ctl log=customer.log
rows=1000 bindarraysize=1000000
sqlldr dss_admin/dss_admin control=customer4.ctl log=customer.log
rows=1000 bindarraysize=1000000
sqlldr dss_admin/dss_admin control=customer5.ctl log=customer.log
rows=1000 bindarraysize=1000000
sqlldr dss_admin/dss_admin control=customer6.ctl log=customer.log
rows=1000 bindarraysize=1000000
sqlldr dss_admin/dss_admin control=customer7.ctl log=customer.log
rows=1000 bindarraysize=1000000
sqlldr dss_admin/dss_admin control=customer8.ctl log=customer.log
rows=1000 bindarraysize=1000000
sqlldr dss_admin/dss_admin control=customer9.ctl log=customer.log
rows=1000 bindarraysize=1000000
sqlldr dss_admin/dss_admin control=customer10.ctl log=customer.log
rows=1000 bindarraysize=1000000

sqlldr dss_admin/dss_admin control=orders1.ctl log=orders.log
rows=1000 bindarraysize=1000000
sqlldr dss_admin/dss_admin control=orders2.ctl log=orders.log
rows=1000 bindarraysize=1000000
sqlldr dss_admin/dss_admin control=orders3.ctl log=orders.log
rows=1000 bindarraysize=1000000
sqlldr dss_admin/dss_admin control=orders4.ctl log=orders.log
rows=1000 bindarraysize=1000000
sqlldr dss_admin/dss_admin control=orders5.ctl log=orders.log
rows=1000 bindarraysize=1000000
sqlldr dss_admin/dss_admin control=orders6.ctl log=orders.log
rows=1000 bindarraysize=1000000
sqlldr dss_admin/dss_admin control=orders7.ctl log=orders.log
rows=1000 bindarraysize=1000000
sqlldr dss_admin/dss_admin control=orders8.ctl log=orders.log
rows=1000 bindarraysize=1000000
sqlldr dss_admin/dss_admin control=orders9.ctl log=orders.log
rows=1000 bindarraysize=1000000
sqlldr dss_admin/dss_admin control=orders10.ctl log=orders.log
rows=1000 bindarraysize=1000000


sqlldr dss_admin/dss_admin control=lineitem1.ctl log=lineitem.log
rows=1000 bindarraysize=1000000
sqlldr dss_admin/dss_admin control=lineitem2.ctl log=lineitem.log
rows=1000 bindarraysize=1000000
sqlldr dss_admin/dss_admin control=lineitem3.ctl log=lineitem.log
rows=1000 bindarraysize=1000000
sqlldr dss_admin/dss_admin control=lineitem4.ctl log=lineitem.log
rows=1000 bindarraysize=1000000
sqlldr dss_admin/dss_admin control=lineitem5.ctl log=lineitem.log
rows=1000 bindarraysize=1000000
sqlldr dss_admin/dss_admin control=lineitem6.ctl log=lineitem.log
rows=1000 bindarraysize=1000000
sqlldr dss_admin/dss_admin control=lineitem7.ctl log=lineitem.log
rows=1000 bindarraysize=1000000
sqlldr dss_admin/dss_admin control=lineitem8.ctl log=lineitem.log
rows=1000 bindarraysize=1000000
```

```
sqlldr dss_admin/dss_admin control=lineitem9.ctl log=lineitem.log
rows=1000 bindarraysize=1000000
sqlldr dss_admin/dss_admin control=lineitem10.ctl log=lineitem.log
rows=1000 bindarraysize=1000000
date
```

16. Once the database was built and loaded with data, the indexes were created using a manually generated index creation script. The full script is located in Appendix A.

17. The index build completed the data loading. Next the schema was analyzed to ensure that the cost-based optimizer (CBO) had proper statistics with which to determine proper query paths. Here is the script used to generate the statistics.

🖫 Analyze.sql

```
-- ****************************************************
-- Copyright © 2003 by Rampant TechPress
-- This script is free for non-commercial purposes
-- with no warranties.  Use at your own risk.
--
-- To license this script for a commercial purpose,
-- contact info@rampant.cc
-- ****************************************************

spool analyze.log
select to_char(sysdate,'dd-mon-yy hh24:mi.ss') from dual;
execute dbms_stats.gather_schema_stats('DSS_ADMIN');
select to_char(sysdate,'dd-mon-yy hh24:mi.ss') from dual;
spool off
exit;
```

18. After the database was prepared, the *qgen* utility was utilized to generate the 22 standard queries for the TPCH Benchmark. A complete set of which is listed in Appendix B. For the most part the 22 scripts could be run as is, however there were SQLServer specific function calls which had to be altered into their Oracle counterparts.

```
$ export DSS_PATH=/home/oracle/benchmark/gen_queries
$ export DSS_QUERY=/home/oracle/benchmark/queries
$ qgen>/home/oracle/benchmark/gen_queries/queries.lst
```

19. Once the database was built, loaded, indexed and analyzed, the 22 standard queries were run against the database for

various configurations of temp, redo, archive logging and memory configurations.

20. After completing the test on the SSD architecture, the database was dropped and rebuilt using the above procedures on the SCSI/ATA drives

    a. Rebuild indexes on the SCSI/ATA database using the standard scripts.

    b. Re-analyzed the SCSI/ATA database DSS_SCHEMA using the standard script.

    c. Re-ran the 22 standard queries against the SCSI/ATA database for various configurations of temp, redo, data, archive logging and memory configurations.

    d. Compiled and analyzed all results and generated report.

The above methodology proved flexible enough to deal with loss of the SCSI array, require rebuilds due to power outages and several other situations which were encountered during the SCSI/ATA testing.

Conclusion

The total methodology boils down to several basic steps:

1. Build the SDD database

2. Load the database

3. Run tests

4. Repeat for SCSI/ATA database

5. Compile and analyze results

While not overly complex, it is long and tedious work. Compiling the results was especially challenging given that some queries where actually multi-part.

In the next chapter, the actual statistics resulting from the initial build will be reviewed, as well as indexing and setup of the test environment and how these results relate to the SSD testing itself.

Setup for Testing

The Real Work

Of course, after choosing the benchmark and the methodology, now comes the real work. This next chapter covers the actual setup and loading of the database in preparation for running the tests.

It's important not to overload the benchmark server

Server Configuration

The database server was provided by TMS configured with RedHat AS 3.0:

```
[oracle@amd43 oracle]$ uname -a
Linux amd43 2.4.21-4.ELsmp #1 SMP Fri Oct 3 17:52:56 EDT 2003 i686
i686 i386 GNU/Linux
```

The kernel parameter configuration of the Linux system was altered to the suggested Oracle configuration for Oracle9i using a startup script loaded into run levels 3, 4, 5 and 6 using the *chkconfig* Linux supplied utility. The actual startup script is listed below:

🖫 **kconfig**

```
-- ****************************************************
-- Copyright © 2003 by Rampant TechPress
-- This script is free for non-commercial purposes
-- with no warranties.  Use at your own risk.
--
-- To license this script for a commercial purpose,
-- contact info@rampant.cc
-- ****************************************************

#!/bin/bash
#kconfig shell script
#chkconfig: 3456 80 10
#description: Oracle Kernel Config
# /etc/init.d/kconfig
# Description: Sets various configurations for Oracle
# See how we were called.
case "$1" in
  start|restart)
echo "256 32000 100 128">/proc/sys/kernel/sem
echo "2147483648">/proc/sys/kernel/shmmax
echo "100">/proc/sys/kernel/shmmni
echo "4096">/proc/sys/kernel/shmseg
echo "32767">/proc/sys/kernel/shmvmx
echo "65535">/proc/sys/fs/file-max
;;
  stop)
        ;;
  *)
```

```
        echo "Usage: kconfig {start|stop|restart}"
        exit 1
esac
exit 0
```

Proper server configuration is critical for any benchmark

Other system parameters were left set at their default values. The output result of the Linux *env* command displays the parameter settings.

The env command produces several pages of output! The results are fully listed here in order to show that no Linux tuning parameters that wouldn't be used in a standard environment were used in the configuration.

```
abi.fake_utsname = 0
abi.trace = 0
abi.defhandler_libcso = 68157441
abi.defhandler_lcall7 = 68157441
abi.defhandler_elf = 0
abi.defhandler_coff = 117440515
```

```
dev.parport.parport0.devices.lp.timeslice = 200
dev.parport.parport0.devices.active = none
dev.parport.parport0.modes = PCSPP
dev.parport.parport0.dma = -1
dev.parport.parport0.irq = -1
dev.parport.parport0.base-addr = 888        1912
dev.parport.parport0.spintime = 500
dev.parport.default.spintime = 500
dev.parport.default.timeslice = 200
dev.raid.speed_limit_max = 10000
dev.raid.speed_limit_min = 100
dev.rtc.max-user-freq = 64
debug.rpmarch =
debug.kerneltype =
net.unix.max_dgram_qlen = 10
net.token-ring.rif_timeout = 60000
net.ipv4.ip_conntrack_max = 65536
net.ipv4.conf.eth1.disable_policy = 0
net.ipv4.conf.eth1.disable_xfrm = 0
net.ipv4.conf.eth1.arp_filter = 0
net.ipv4.conf.eth1.tag = 0
net.ipv4.conf.eth1.log_martians = 0
net.ipv4.conf.eth1.bootp_relay = 0
net.ipv4.conf.eth1.medium_id = 0
net.ipv4.conf.eth1.proxy_arp = 0
net.ipv4.conf.eth1.accept_source_route = 1
net.ipv4.conf.eth1.send_redirects = 1
net.ipv4.conf.eth1.rp_filter = 1
net.ipv4.conf.eth1.shared_media = 1
net.ipv4.conf.eth1.secure_redirects = 1
net.ipv4.conf.eth1.accept_redirects = 1
net.ipv4.conf.eth1.mc_forwarding = 0
net.ipv4.conf.eth1.forwarding = 0
net.ipv4.conf.lo.disable_policy = 0
net.ipv4.conf.lo.disable_xfrm = 0
net.ipv4.conf.lo.arp_filter = 0
net.ipv4.conf.lo.tag = 0
net.ipv4.conf.lo.log_martians = 0
net.ipv4.conf.lo.bootp_relay = 0
net.ipv4.conf.lo.medium_id = 0
net.ipv4.conf.lo.proxy_arp = 0
net.ipv4.conf.lo.accept_source_route = 1
net.ipv4.conf.lo.send_redirects = 1
net.ipv4.conf.lo.rp_filter = 1
net.ipv4.conf.lo.shared_media = 1
net.ipv4.conf.lo.secure_redirects = 1
net.ipv4.conf.lo.accept_redirects = 1
net.ipv4.conf.lo.mc_forwarding = 0
net.ipv4.conf.lo.forwarding = 0
net.ipv4.conf.default.disable_policy = 0
net.ipv4.conf.default.disable_xfrm = 0
net.ipv4.conf.default.arp_filter = 0
net.ipv4.conf.default.tag = 0
net.ipv4.conf.default.log_martians = 0
net.ipv4.conf.default.bootp_relay = 0
net.ipv4.conf.default.medium_id = 0
net.ipv4.conf.default.proxy_arp = 0
```

```
net.ipv4.conf.default.accept_source_route = 1
net.ipv4.conf.default.send_redirects = 1
net.ipv4.conf.default.rp_filter = 1
net.ipv4.conf.default.shared_media = 1
net.ipv4.conf.default.secure_redirects = 1
net.ipv4.conf.default.accept_redirects = 1
net.ipv4.conf.default.mc_forwarding = 0
net.ipv4.conf.default.forwarding = 0
net.ipv4.conf.all.disable_policy = 0
net.ipv4.conf.all.disable_xfrm = 0
net.ipv4.conf.all.arp_filter = 0
net.ipv4.conf.all.tag = 0
net.ipv4.conf.all.log_martians = 0
net.ipv4.conf.all.bootp_relay = 0
net.ipv4.conf.all.medium_id = 0
net.ipv4.conf.all.proxy_arp = 0
net.ipv4.conf.all.accept_source_route = 0
net.ipv4.conf.all.send_redirects = 1
net.ipv4.conf.all.rp_filter = 0
net.ipv4.conf.all.shared_media = 1
net.ipv4.conf.all.secure_redirects = 1
net.ipv4.conf.all.accept_redirects = 1
net.ipv4.conf.all.mc_forwarding = 0
net.ipv4.conf.all.forwarding = 0
net.ipv4.neigh.eth1.locktime = 100
net.ipv4.neigh.eth1.proxy_delay = 80
net.ipv4.neigh.eth1.anycast_delay = 100
net.ipv4.neigh.eth1.proxy_qlen = 64
net.ipv4.neigh.eth1.unres_qlen = 3
net.ipv4.neigh.eth1.gc_stale_time = 60
net.ipv4.neigh.eth1.delay_first_probe_time = 5
net.ipv4.neigh.eth1.base_reachable_time = 30
net.ipv4.neigh.eth1.retrans_time = 100
net.ipv4.neigh.eth1.app_solicit = 0
net.ipv4.neigh.eth1.ucast_solicit = 3
net.ipv4.neigh.eth1.mcast_solicit = 3
net.ipv4.neigh.lo.locktime = 100
net.ipv4.neigh.lo.proxy_delay = 80
net.ipv4.neigh.lo.anycast_delay = 100
net.ipv4.neigh.lo.proxy_qlen = 64
net.ipv4.neigh.lo.unres_qlen = 3
net.ipv4.neigh.lo.gc_stale_time = 60
net.ipv4.neigh.lo.delay_first_probe_time = 5
net.ipv4.neigh.lo.base_reachable_time = 30
net.ipv4.neigh.lo.retrans_time = 100
net.ipv4.neigh.lo.app_solicit = 0
net.ipv4.neigh.lo.ucast_solicit = 3
net.ipv4.neigh.lo.mcast_solicit = 3
net.ipv4.neigh.default.gc_thresh3 = 1024
net.ipv4.neigh.default.gc_thresh2 = 512
net.ipv4.neigh.default.gc_thresh1 = 128
net.ipv4.neigh.default.gc_interval = 30
net.ipv4.neigh.default.locktime = 100
net.ipv4.neigh.default.proxy_delay = 80
net.ipv4.neigh.default.anycast_delay = 100
net.ipv4.neigh.default.proxy_qlen = 64
net.ipv4.neigh.default.unres_qlen = 3
```

```
net.ipv4.neigh.default.gc_stale_time = 60
net.ipv4.neigh.default.delay_first_probe_time = 5
net.ipv4.neigh.default.base_reachable_time = 30
net.ipv4.neigh.default.retrans_time = 100
net.ipv4.neigh.default.app_solicit = 0
net.ipv4.neigh.default.ucast_solicit = 3
net.ipv4.neigh.default.mcast_solicit = 3
net.ipv4.ipfrag_secret_interval = 600
net.ipv4.tcp_low_latency = 0
net.ipv4.tcp_frto = 0
net.ipv4.tcp_tw_reuse = 0
net.ipv4.icmp_ratemask = 6168
net.ipv4.icmp_ratelimit = 100
net.ipv4.tcp_adv_win_scale = 2
net.ipv4.tcp_app_win = 31
net.ipv4.tcp_rmem = 4096       87380     174760
net.ipv4.tcp_wmem = 4096       16384     131072
net.ipv4.tcp_mem = 195584   196096  196608
net.ipv4.tcp_dsack = 1
net.ipv4.tcp_ecn = 0
net.ipv4.tcp_reordering = 3
net.ipv4.tcp_fack = 1
net.ipv4.tcp_orphan_retries = 0
net.ipv4.inet_peer_gc_maxtime = 120
net.ipv4.inet_peer_gc_mintime = 10
net.ipv4.inet_peer_maxttl = 600
net.ipv4.inet_peer_minttl = 120
net.ipv4.inet_peer_threshold = 65664
net.ipv4.igmp_max_memberships = 20
net.ipv4.route.secret_interval = 600
net.ipv4.route.min_adv_mss = 256
net.ipv4.route.min_pmtu = 552
net.ipv4.route.mtu_expires = 600
net.ipv4.route.gc_elasticity = 8
net.ipv4.route.error_burst = 500
net.ipv4.route.error_cost = 100
net.ipv4.route.redirect_silence = 2048
net.ipv4.route.redirect_number = 9
net.ipv4.route.redirect_load = 2
net.ipv4.route.gc_interval = 60
net.ipv4.route.gc_timeout = 300
net.ipv4.route.gc_min_interval = 0
net.ipv4.route.max_size = 524288
net.ipv4.route.gc_thresh = 32768
net.ipv4.route.max_delay = 10
net.ipv4.route.min_delay = 2
net.ipv4.icmp_ignore_bogus_error_responses = 0
net.ipv4.icmp_echo_ignore_broadcasts = 0
net.ipv4.icmp_echo_ignore_all = 0
net.ipv4.ip_local_port_range = 32768        61000
net.ipv4.tcp_max_syn_backlog = 1024
net.ipv4.tcp_rfc1337 = 0
net.ipv4.tcp_stdurg = 0
net.ipv4.tcp_abort_on_overflow = 0
net.ipv4.tcp_tw_recycle = 0
net.ipv4.tcp_syncookies = 0
net.ipv4.tcp_fin_timeout = 60
```

```
net.ipv4.tcp_retries2 = 15
net.ipv4.tcp_retries1 = 3
net.ipv4.tcp_keepalive_intvl = 75
net.ipv4.tcp_keepalive_probes = 9
net.ipv4.tcp_keepalive_time = 7200
net.ipv4.ipfrag_time = 30
net.ipv4.ip_dynaddr = 0
net.ipv4.ipfrag_low_thresh = 196608
net.ipv4.ipfrag_high_thresh = 262144
net.ipv4.tcp_max_tw_buckets = 180000
net.ipv4.tcp_max_orphans = 32768
net.ipv4.tcp_synack_retries = 5
net.ipv4.tcp_syn_retries = 5
net.ipv4.ip_nonlocal_bind = 0
net.ipv4.ip_no_pmtu_disc = 0
net.ipv4.ip_autoconfig = 0
net.ipv4.ip_default_ttl = 64
net.ipv4.ip_forward = 0
net.ipv4.tcp_retrans_collapse = 1
net.ipv4.tcp_sack = 1
net.ipv4.tcp_window_scaling = 1
net.ipv4.tcp_timestamps = 1
net.core.divert_version = 0.46
net.core.hot_list_length = 128
net.core.optmem_max = 10240
net.core.message_burst = 50
net.core.message_cost = 5
net.core.mod_cong = 290
net.core.lo_cong = 100
net.core.no_cong = 20
net.core.no_cong_thresh = 20
net.core.netdev_max_backlog = 300
net.core.dev_weight = 64
net.core.rmem_default = 65535
net.core.wmem_default = 65535
net.core.rmem_max = 131071
net.core.wmem_max = 131071
vm.inactive_clean_percent = 5
vm.dcache_priority = 0
vm.hugetlb_pool = 0
vm.max_map_count = 65536
vm.max-readahead = 31
vm.min-readahead = 3
vm.page-cluster = 3
vm.pagetable_cache = 25      50
vm.kswapd = 512      32      8
vm.pagecache = 1     15      100
vm.overcommit_ratio = 50
vm.overcommit_memory = 0
vm.bdflush = 50      500      0      0      500      3000      80      50
     0
kernel.sercons_esc = -1
kernel.overflowgid = 65534
kernel.overflowuid = 65534
kernel.random.uuid = 527df12c-992f-4df7-8e05-9ea6340d7730
kernel.random.boot_id = 437956b8-e8c5-40d6-be5c-5df391ab3975
kernel.random.write_wakeup_threshold = 128
```

```
kernel.random.read_wakeup_threshold = 8
kernel.random.entropy_avail = 4096
kernel.random.poolsize = 512
kernel.pid_max = 32768
kernel.threads-max = 14336
kernel.cad_pid = 1
kernel.sysrq-timer = 10
kernel.sysrq-sticky = 0
kernel.sysrq-key = 84
kernel.sysrq = 0
kernel.sem = 250     32000   32      128
kernel.msgmnb = 16384
kernel.msgmni = 16
kernel.msgmax = 8192
kernel.shmmni = 4096
kernel.shmall = 2097152
kernel.shmmax = 33554432
kernel.rtsig-max = 1024
kernel.rtsig-nr = 0
kernel.acct = 4      2       30
kernel.hotplug = /sbin/hotplug
kernel.modprobe = /sbin/modprobe
kernel.printk = 6    4       1       7
kernel.ctrl-alt-del = 0
kernel.real-root-dev = 256
kernel.task_size = -1073741824
kernel.cap-bound = -257
kernel.tainted = 0
kernel.core_pattern = core
kernel.core_setuid_ok = 0
kernel.core_uses_pid = 1
kernel.print_fatal_signals = 0
kernel.panic_on_oops = 1
kernel.panic = 0
kernel.domainname = (none)
kernel.hostname = AMD43
kernel.version = #1 SMP Mon Feb 9 22:08:44 EST 2004
kernel.osrelease = 2.4.21-9.0.1.ELsmp
kernel.ostype = Linux
fs.quota.syncs = 9
fs.quota.free_dquots = 0
fs.quota.allocated_dquots = 0
fs.quota.cache_hits = 0
fs.quota.writes = 0
fs.quota.reads = 0
fs.quota.drops = 0
fs.quota.lookups = 0
fs.aio-pinned = 0
fs.aio-max-pinned = 258044
fs.aio-max-size = 131072
fs.aio-max-nr = 65536
fs.aio-nr = 0
fs.lease-break-time = 45
fs.dir-notify-enable = 1
fs.leases-enable = 1
fs.overflowgid = 65534
fs.overflowuid = 65534
```

```
fs.dentry-state = 997      519    45     0     0     0
fs.file-max = 412870
fs.file-nr = 1032   148    412870
fs.inode-state = 1585      808    0      0     0     0     0
fs.inode-nr = 1585  808
```

Admittedly better performance could have been obtained from adjusting various system parameters, but this wasn't a system tuning operation. In fact, from experience many sites take the defaults rather than tweaking the operating system for the optimal performance, so leaving them at their defaults makes the test more realistic.

In conclusion, other than normal Oracle related settings, no other changes where made to the standard Linux RedHat3.0 environment. Now it is time to review the setup of the various disk arrays.

Disk Configurations

As previously stated, a TMS RAMSan, a SCSI disk array, and an ATA disk array were utilized during tests. If this were a full disclosure benchmark, it would be necessary to divulge the manufacturers, prices, and other details about the various arrays. Since this is not a full benchmark, the important characteristics of the disk array will be provided without divulging the manufacturers since they were good enough to lend their equipment for the tests. The specifications for the various disk and SSD equipment used are as follows.

- The Texas Memory Systems solid state disk array, a 64 Gigabyte RamSan 320 was presented as one large disk. The RamSan has no stripes, mirrors or other physical specifications other than those created by the volume creation commands presented before. The RamSan has built-in backup capabilities in case of loss of power and is built using state-of-the-art high-speed ECC memory chips.

- The SCSI array used in initial testing consisted of 2-36 Gigabyte 10,000 RPM Seagate Cheetah disks striped at 128K.

- The ATA array used in final testing consisted of 7-200 Gigabyte 7,200 RPM 133 disks. The disks were striped n 64K stripes.

- The disk HBA interface cards were QlogicQLA2342 2-Gigabit fibre channel.

The output of the *dmesg* command show the actual system disk configurations for the first part of the test using the SCSI drives.

```
scsi(1): Topology - (N_Port-to-N_Port), Host Loop address 0x1
  Vendor: TMS       Model: FC65          Rev: 1.4b
  Type:   Direct-Access                  ANSI SCSI revision: 04
Starting timer : 0 0
blk: queue f6e24e18, I/O limit 4095Mb (mask 0xffffffff)
scsi(0:0:0:0): Enabled tagged queuing, queue depth 32.
Starting timer : 0 0
  Vendor: (omitted by request)  Model: (omitted) FC RAID    Rev:
3.03
  Type:   Direct-Access                  ANSI SCSI revision: 03
Starting timer : 0 0
blk: queue f6e24c18, I/O limit 4095Mb (mask 0xffffffff)
scsi(1:0:0:0): Enabled tagged queuing, queue depth 32.
Attached scsi disk sda at scsi0, channel 0, id 0, lun 0
Attached scsi disk sdb at scsi1, channel 0, id 0, lun 0
SCSI device sda: 134217728 512-byte hdwr sectors (68719 MB)
 sda: unknown partition table
SCSI device sdb: 143360000 512-byte hdwr sectors (73400 MB)
 sdb: unknown partition table
```

Other than showing a different device, the listing for the ATA based disk array was identical to the listing for *sdb* above.

Other than the RAMSan array, these are standard off-the-shelf components configured as they would be for use in Oracle shops worldwide. The next topic is the network configuration.

Network Configurations

Standard network configuration was used. The NIC cards where 1 Gigabit and, along with the network switches, were commercial off-the-shelf variety in use in Oracle shops worldwide. All network settings were shown in the previous section showing the output from the Linux *env* command.

Proper networking is critical!

While for this test, network configuration wasn't as critical as for a Real Application Cluster test for instance, it was none the less important to have components that would be standard components for most Oracle shops.

The Orac database setup will be covered next.

Database Configuration:

The database was setup using a standard set of initialization parameters as shown below, which is a capture of the Oracle *show parameter* command with no options specified. As with the *env* shown in the section on server configuration, the parameter listing for an Oracle database is several pages long. However, the point here was to show that no special tricks and no undocumented parameters were used to make the database behave in anyway other than a normal Oracle9i database.

```
NAME                                   TYPE        VALUE
------------------------------------   ----------  --------------------

O7_DICTIONARY_ACCESSIBILITY            boolean     FALSE
aq_tm_processes                        integer     1
archive_lag_target                     integer     0
audit_file_dest                        string      ?/rdbms/audit
audit_sys_operations                   boolean     FALSE
audit_trail                            string      NONE
background_core_dump                   string      partial
background_dump_dest                   string
/home/oracle/admin/dss/bdump
backup_tape_io_slaves                  boolean     FALSE
bitmap_merge_area_size                 integer     1048576
blank_trimming                         boolean     FALSE
circuits                               integer     170
commit_point_strength                  integer     1
compatible                             string      9.2.0.0.0
control_file_record_keep_time          integer     7
control_files                          string
/home/oracle/oradata/dss/CONTR
                                                   OL01.CTL,
/home/oracle/oradata
                                                   /dss/CONTROL02.CTL,
/home/orac

le/oradata/dss/CONTROL03.CTL
core_dump_dest                         string
/home/oracle/admin/dss/cdump
cpu_count                              integer     2
create_bitmap_area_size                integer     8388608
cursor_sharing                         string      EXACT
cursor_space_for_time                  boolean     FALSE
db_block_checking                      boolean     FALSE
db_block_checksum                      boolean     TRUE
db_block_size                          integer     16384
db_cache_advice                        string      ON
db_cache_size                          big integer 1073741824
db_file_multiblock_read_count          integer     16
db_files                               integer     200
db_name                                string      dss
db_writer_processes                    integer     1
dblink_encrypt_login                   boolean     FALSE
dg_broker_config_file1                 string      ?/dbs/dr1@.dat
dg_broker_config_file2                 string      ?/dbs/dr2@.dat
dg_broker_start                        boolean     FALSE
disk_asynch_io                         boolean     TRUE
```

dispatchers	string	(PROTOCOL=TCP)
(SERVICE=dssXDB)		
distributed_lock_timeout	integer	60
dml_locks	integer	748
drs_start	boolean	FALSE
enqueue_resources	integer	968
fast_start_io_target	integer	0
fast_start_mttr_target	integer	300
fast_start_parallel_rollback	string	LOW
file_mapping	boolean	FALSE
filesystemio_options	string	none
global_names	boolean	FALSE
hash_area_size	integer	1048576
hash_join_enabled	boolean	TRUE
hi_shared_memory_address	integer	0
hs_autoregister	boolean	TRUE
instance_name	string	dss
java_max_sessionspace_size	integer	0
java_pool_size	big integer	33554432
java_soft_sessionspace_limit	integer	0
job_queue_processes	integer	10
large_pool_size	big integer	16777216
lock_sga	boolean	FALSE
log_archive_start	boolean	FALSE
log_buffer	integer	524288
log_checkpoint_interval	integer	0
log_checkpoint_timeout	integer	1800
log_checkpoints_to_alert	boolean	FALSE
log_parallelism	integer	1
logmnr_max_persistent_sessions	integer	1
max_commit_propagation_delay	integer	700
max_dispatchers	integer	5
max_dump_file_size	string	UNLIMITED
max_enabled_roles	integer	30
max_rollback_segments	integer	37
max_shared_servers	integer	20
mts_circuits	integer	170
mts_dispatchers	string	(PROTOCOL=TCP)
(SERVICE=dssXDB)		
mts_max_dispatchers	integer	5
mts_max_servers	integer	20
mts_multiple_listeners	boolean	FALSE
mts_servers	integer	1
mts_service	string	dss
mts_sessions	integer	165
nls_language	string	AMERICAN
nls_length_semantics	string	BYTE
nls_nchar_conv_excp	string	FALSE
nls_territory	string	AMERICA
object_cache_max_size_percent	integer	10
object_cache_optimal_size	integer	102400
olap_page_pool_size	integer	33554432
open_cursors	integer	300
open_links	integer	4
open_links_per_instance	integer	4
optimizer_dynamic_sampling	integer	1
optimizer_features_enable	string	9.2.0

```
optimizer_index_caching            integer      0
optimizer_index_cost_adj           integer      100
optimizer_max_permutations         integer      2000
optimizer_mode                     string       CHOOSE
oracle_trace_collection_path       string       ?/otrace/admin/cdf
oracle_trace_collection_size       integer      5242880
oracle_trace_enable                boolean      FALSE
oracle_trace_facility_name         string       oracled
oracle_trace_facility_path         string       ?/otrace/admin/fdf
os_authent_prefix                  string       ops$
os_roles                           boolean      FALSE
parallel_adaptive_multi_user       boolean      FALSE
parallel_automatic_tuning          boolean      FALSE
parallel_execution_message_size    integer      2148
parallel_max_servers               integer      5
parallel_min_percent               integer      0
parallel_min_servers               integer      0
parallel_server                    boolean      FALSE
parallel_server_instances          integer      1
parallel_threads_per_cpu           integer      2
partition_view_enabled             boolean      FALSE
pga_aggregate_target               big integer  2147483648
plsql_compiler_flags               string       INTERPRETED
plsql_native_library_subdir_count  integer      0
plsql_v2_compatibility             boolean      FALSE
pre_page_sga                       boolean      FALSE
processes                          integer      150
query_rewrite_enabled              string       FALSE
query_rewrite_integrity            string       enforced
read_only_open_delayed             boolean      FALSE
recovery_parallelism               integer      0
remote_archive_enable              string       true
remote_dependencies_mode           string       TIMESTAMP
remote_login_passwordfile          string       EXCLUSIVE
remote_os_authent                  boolean      FALSE
remote_os_roles                    boolean      FALSE
replication_dependency_tracking    boolean      TRUE
resource_limit                     boolean      FALSE
row_locking                        string       always
serial_reuse                       string       DISABLE
serializable                       boolean      FALSE
service_names                      string       dss
session_cached_cursors             integer      0
session_max_open_files             integer      10
sessions                           integer      170
sga_max_size                       big integer  1310862512
shadow_core_dump                   string       partial
shared_memory_address              integer      0
shared_pool_reserved_size          big integer  2516582
shared_pool_size                   big integer  50331648
shared_server_sessions             integer      165
shared_servers                     integer      1
sort_area_retained_size            integer      0
sort_area_size                     integer      524288
spfile                             string       ?/dbs/spfile@.ora
sql92_security                     boolean      FALSE
sql_trace                          boolean      FALSE
```

```
sql_version                          string      NATIVE
standby_archive_dest                 string      ?/dbs/arch
standby_file_management              string      MANUAL
star_transformation_enabled          string      FALSE
statistics_level                     string      TYPICAL
tape_asynch_io                       boolean     TRUE
thread                               integer     0
timed_os_statistics                  integer     0
timed_statistics                     boolean     TRUE
trace_enabled                        boolean     TRUE
transaction_auditing                 boolean     TRUE
transactions                         integer     187
transactions_per_rollback_segment    integer     5
undo_management                      string      AUTO
undo_retention                       integer     10800
undo_suppress_errors                 boolean     FALSE
undo_tablespace                      string      UNDOTBS
use_indirect_data_buffers            boolean     FALSE
user_dump_dest                       string
/home/oracle/admin/dss/udump
workarea_size_policy                 string      AUTO
```

Following the initial load of the 9.2.0.1 base product, Oracle patch set 3095277 was applied to bring the database software to release 9.2.0.4. The Oracle Universal Installer was used to perform the initial installation and patching.

Once the database was installed and patched to the proper release level, the Oracle supplied database creation assistant (*dbca*) utility was used to generate a set of database creation scripts. The decision was made to utilize scripts because the same exact set of scripts could then be used and documented to create all test databases.

Using the *dbca* created scripts, the database was created in *noarchivelog* mode and the tables were created using a standard table create script. *nologging* was specified for the initial data load, index builds and series of tests.

At this point in the process, there is a standard Oracle9i database, patched appropriately to release 9.2.0.4 and configured as a normal database would be configured in any Oracle shop in the world. The required tablespaces, user tables, and base tables for the test have been built. Data loading is next.

Data Loading

The data loading into the two configurations, SSD and SCSI/ATA, was performed using the SQLLoader script previously shown in Chapter 2. The dependency of the various tables was determined and the load script created to avoid data dependency issues. Each of the flat files (10 each for the large tables) was loaded in numerical sequence and the timing data recorded. The data loading was used as a test of the insert speed of the various configurations.

Overall the load speeds for the SCSI 2-disk array and the ATA 7-Disk array were found to be nearly identical. Only one set of statistics from the ATA second series of loads will be compared. Figure 3.1 shows a graph of load time comparisons for the PARTSUPP table between the SSD and SCSI/ATA data loads. The average speed improvement for data loading was 30% for SSD over SCSI/ATA arrays.

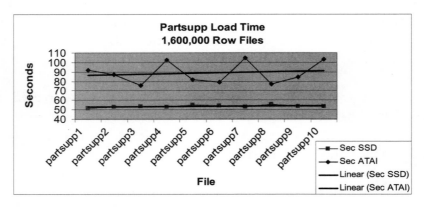

Figure 3.1: *Partsupp Load Time Comparison*

The examples used are the *partsupp* table loads, each consisting of 1.6 million rows. The complete results for the *partsupp* table are in Table 3.1.

LOAD FILE	ROW COUNT	SSD LOAD SEC	ROWS PER SEC	SSD/SCSI
partsupp1	1600000	51.58	31019.775	0.559679
partsupp2	1600000	52.88	30257.186	0.60545
partsupp3	1600000	53.53	29889.781	0.707414
partsupp4	1600000	52.47	30493.615	0.512853
partsupp5	1600000	54.88	29154.519	0.674119
partsupp6	1600000	54.43	29395.554	0.688377
partsupp7	1600000	52.94	30222.894	0.505635
partsupp8	1600000	55.56	28797.696	0.721746
partsupp9	1600000	53.13	30114.813	0.628906
partsupp10	1600000	53.39	29968.159	0.516145

LOAD FILE	ROW COUNT	SCSI LOAD SEC	ROWS PER SEC
partsupp1	1600000	92.16	17361.11
partsupp2	1600000	87.34	18319.21
partsupp3	1600000	75.67	21144.44
partsupp4	1600000	102.31	15638.74
partsupp5	1600000	81.41	19653.61
partsupp6	1600000	79.07	20235.23
partsupp7	1600000	104.7	15281.76
partsupp8	1600000	76.98	20784.62
partsupp9	1600000	84.48	18939.39
partsupp10	1600000	103.44	15467.9

Table 3.1: *Comparison of partsupp Table Loads between SSD and SCSI/ATA*

The rows per second insert rate is shown in Table 3.1 and also reflects the performance improvements as demonstrated by the data represented in the graph in Figure 3.2.

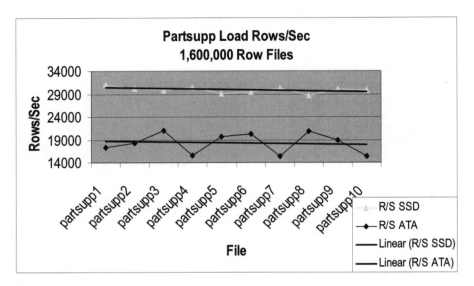

Figure 3.2: *Example Rows per Second Comparison*

The SSD drives loaded 66 percent more rows per second. Although this doesn't correlate to the 30 percent speed improvement shown in Figure 3.1, the 30% (40% maximum) improvement does correlate with the findings from other testers listed in Chapter 1. The complete data showing all load statistics are provided in Appendix C.

Figure 3.3 shows the average load times for each table compared between the SSD and ATA loads.

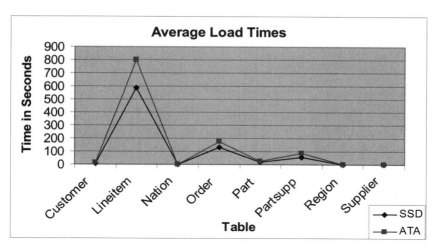

Figure 3.2: *Average Table Load Time Comparison*

As can be seen, with the possible exception of the nation and region tables the average load time for the SSD load was 30% less than the average load time for ATA. This data is shown in tabular form in Table 2.

TABLE NAME	SSD AVERAGE LOAD TIME	ATA AVERAGE LOAD TIME
Customer	8.61	12.35
Lineitem	587.80	802.50
Nation	0.07	0.05
Order	132.34	175.02
Part	15.66	21.91
Partsupp	53.48	88.76
Region	0.12	0.08
Supplier	0.60	0.82

Table 3.2: *Average Load Times Per Table*

This performance was seen across the board with the exception of the two inconsequential small tables which can be disregarded.

Figure 3.3 shows the average rows per second during loading for all tables for both SSD and SCSI.

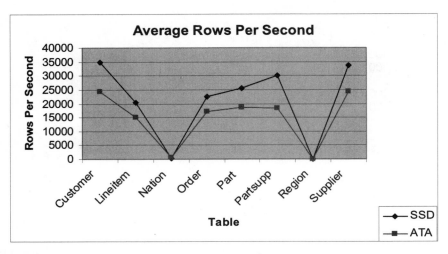

Figure 3.3: *Average Rows Per Second for all Tables*

SSD is fastest for data loads!

Figure 3.3 shows graphically that SSD loads rows considerably faster than ATA drives The reason for the mismatch between row loading efficiency (up to 60%) and the difference in load times (up to 40 %) is still not clear but could be due to the primary key index insert time which may not have been properly captured in the statistics. Table 3.3 shows the actual values that support Figure 3.3.

TABLE	SSD R/S	ATA R/S
Customer	34892.81	24493.74
Lineitem	20415.51	15009.14
Nation	357.14	500.00
Order	22675.75	17254.85
Part	25570.33	18574.75
Partsupp	29931.40	18282.60
Region	41.67	62.50
Supplier	33614.46	24489.11

Table 3.3: *Rows Per Second Averages*

In conclusion, the SSD array outperformed the SCSI and ATA arrays in load time by an average of 30%. This means that for a data load sequence that may take 3 hours on a SCSI or ATA array, it would only require close to 2 hours on a SSD array. In addition the rows per second load rate was nearly 60% faster. So, in a situation where there are no other factors such as primary key index builds, the actual load time may be even better than the 30% average peak performance shown.

Next, it is time to cover the index build efficiency.

Index Builds

The next phase of the database build was the application of indexes. The index builds were also scripted and the times for each index build logged. These times demonstrate update performance via updates to indexes. Figure 3.4 shows the comparisons for all index builds between the SSD and SCSI/ATA databases on the *dss_admin* schema.

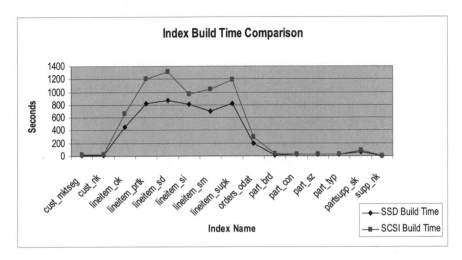

Figure 3.4: *Index Build Time Comparisons*

As with the insert testing the updates into the SSD array required 30% less time than the updates into the SCSI/ATA arrays. This compares favorably with other researchers results. The complete index build comparison statistics are shown in Appendix C.

Again, this shows that for update based activity and complex searching and sorting such is done with indexing, an SSD array will outperform standard technologies by at least 30%.

In the next phase, another complex task will be covered, the analyze runs to capture object statistics for the cost based optimizer.

Analyze Runs

The analyze runs were scripted and the logs captured. Unfortunately the log from the SSD run was overwritten by a subsequent log and was lost. However, the elapsed time was calculated for both the SCSI and ATA runs. The SCSI analyze run completed in 126.76 seconds. The ATA analyze run required 149.12 seconds to complete.

The percentage difference between these two runs is 15% with the SCSI analyze requiring only 85% of the time required by the ATA architecture to complete the analysis of all schema tables and indexes. The logs from the SCSI and ATA runs are shown in below.

```
SQL*Plus: Release 9.2.0.4.0 - Production on Wed Jun 2 12:29:34 2004

Copyright (c) 1982, 2002, Oracle Corporation.  All rights reserved.
Connected to:

Oracle9i Enterprise Edition Release 9.2.0.4.0 - Production
With the Partitioning, OLAP and Oracle Data Mining options
JServer Release 9.2.0.4.0 - Production


TO_CHAR(SYSDATE,'D
------------------
02-jun-04 12:29.34


PL/SQL procedure successfully completed.


TO_CHAR(SYSDATE,'D
------------------
02-jun-04 14:36.10

Disconnected from Oracle9i Enterprise Edition Release 9.2.0.4.0 -
Production
With the Partitioning, OLAP and Oracle Data Mining options
JServer Release 9.2.0.4.0 - Production

SQL*Plus: Release 9.2.0.4.0 - Production on Wed Jun 29 13:27:03 2004

Copyright (c) 1982, 2002, Oracle Corporation.  All rights reserved.
Connected to:
```

```
Oracle9i Enterprise Edition Release 9.2.0.4.0 - Production
With the Partitioning, OLAP and Oracle Data Mining options
JServer Release 9.2.0.4.0 - Production

TO_CHAR(SYSDATE,'D
------------------
29-jun-04 13:27.03


PL/SQL procedure successfully completed.


TO_CHAR(SYSDATE,'D
------------------
29-jun-04 15:56.15

Disconnected from Oracle9i Enterprise Edition Release 9.2.0.4.0 -
Production
With the Partitioning, OLAP and Oracle Data Mining options
JServer Release 9.2.0.4.0 - Production
```

With the completion of analyze, the database is ready to be tested.

Conclusion

Based on the database creation and loading a hypothesis can be made that there should be at least a 30% performance improvement in subsequent tests. Across the board the SSD array out loaded, out inserted, and out updated the SCSI and ATA arrays.

Now it is time to look at the actual testing results for the DSS benchmark queries.

Testing SSD Verses ATA Performance

Introduction

In this chapter the actual test results form a series of TPCH benchmark queries for both SSD and ATA arrays will be reviewed along with an Oracle9i, 9.2.0.4 database. ATA is the abbreviation for IBM PC/AT Attachment. The "AT" is IBM's abbreviation for "advanced technology." This terminology was first coined in 1984 to describe the integrated disk electronics or IDE drives in PC based hardware.

The wrong choice of I/O subsystem can affect performance

Query Processing

The *qgen* program produces 22 example DSS (Decision Support System) queries. The queries use aggregation, sub-queries, order-bys and group bys to simulate the processing in a DSS environment. The queries were placed into a single file and run back-to-back in the tests. STATSPACK and custom scripts were used to monitor the database.

A simple SQLPlus connection to the database was implemented through standard TCPIP connections. In fact, remote connections were utilized from several different locations during the testing time frame to monitor and re-run queries as required. A testing harness for use with the Linux *nohup* utility was required. This test harness consisted of a simple command to call *sqlplus* with our pre-built set of queries:

```
#! /bin/bash
set +x
/home/oracle/bin/sqlplus dss_admin/dss_admin @queries_scsi.lst
```

This test harness was called *run_ssd_queries.sh* or *run_scsi_queries.sh* and was executed using the *nohup* command:

```
nohup ./run_ssd_queries.sh &
```

The use of *nohup* generates a *nohup.out* log file which can be used to see the progress of the various queries and also to capture a detailed log of the test events.

While the SSD runs were completed with single launches of the test harness, the SCSI and ATA runs often required restarts as a result of failure. The *nohup* command, unless instructed to do otherwise, appends new runs to the previous *nohup.out*. Thus, even with the stop/start nature of the SCSI and ATA testing a complete record was still obtained.

Oracle Solid State Disk Tuning

Now, the actual results from the tests.

SSD Results

In the SSD test runs the following configurations were tested:

- Base run to load buffers
- No logging on all tables and no archive log setting
- No logging on all tables with archive logging
- Logging and archive logging

Looking at Figure 4.1 notice that the SSD runs showed very constant times for all the various configurations after query 8 was run in the base load run 1. This type of profile recurred after a shutdown startup, as can be seen in the graph in Figure 4.1. The entire set of 7 total runs only required 3 days to process. It should also be noted that these were not run back-to-back but as time allowed. Figure 4.1 shows the comparisons of the various SSD configurations.

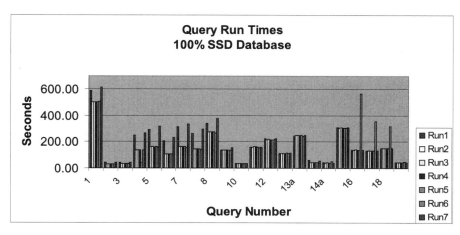

Figure 4.1: *SSD Query Run Times*

Figure 4.1 shows where query number 1, the poorest performing query in its worst run which was run number 7, only required just over 600 seconds to complete. The complete query timings are shown in Table 4.1. Run 6, with archive logging turned on, showed nearly identical query timing results, as compared with previous runs, until the next-to-last three queries.

SSD query	Run1	Run2	Run3	Run4	Run5	Run6	Run7
1	589.94	501.53	502.47	500.54	501.06	507.31	615.21
2	42.24	30.83	30.76	30.44	30.37	30.55	43.18
3	41.55	34.72	35.54	34.83	35.49	35.35	40.86
4	249.30	139.02	139.30	139.42	42.04	136.11	267.70
5	292.28	161.48	162.43	160.54	161.17	158.40	317.08
6	205.12	107.87	109.20	108.88	108.78	107.37	230.25
7	314.09	161.59	162.83	162.01	162.14	156.74	334.97
7a	263.43	144.45	145.12	145.42	144.85	139.88	297.13
8	340.17	272.98	274.20	273.95	273.32	267.27	379.45
9	137.69	137.40	138.78	137.62	138.40	134.25	154.53
10	35.20	35.46	35.72	35.51	35.49	35.28	36.19
11	157.74	159.13	161.64	161.27	160.43	154.48	160.75
12	224.77	215.71	217.33	214.72	215.66	214.58	225.20
13	113.01	113.16	113.79	113.76	113.93	111.85	114.70
13a	246.45	248.79	250.66	249.36	250.39	238.84	249.17
14	57.98	44.32	42.82	41.95	42.04	42.19	54.56
14a	42.49	40.66	40.91	40.50	40.34	50.65	39.86
15	309.07	306.37	308.89	306.73	306.27	305.89	307.92
16	138.37	138.70	140.02	138.65	139.12	565.86	138.11
17	133.08	133.53	134.41	133.71	133.36	355.08	132.71
18	149.93	150.41	150.93	150.86	150.56	319.14	149.90
19	43.58	44.03	44.44	43.41	43.19	47.45	43.35
Total	4127.48	3322.14	3342.19	3324.08	3228.40	4114.52	4332.78

Table 4.1: *Raw data from the SSD Query Runs*

After a restart, query 7 showed similar performance to run 1, even with archive logging turned on, and the three poorly

Oracle Solid State Disk Tuning

performing queries, relative to the other SSD runs, returned to "normal" performance levels.

When using the SSD array the use of logging and archive logging had little or no affect on performance.

Summary of Findings

SSD performance is consistent and the SSD array performed consistently well during the tests. After some initial tweaks to undo tablespace and temporary tablespace sizes, which were subsequently carried over into the SCSI and ATA testing, all SSD test runs were completed without notable incident or issue.

Initial runs after restart of the instance showed poorer performance than subsequent runs. This is expected due to data loading into the Oracle SGA buffers. Changes to the *archivelogging* status of the database or table, and index level logging when logs were written to the SSD array had no measurable effect on SSD performance.

The next section examines SCSI and ATA performance.

SCSI and ATA Runs

The SCSI runs required 58 days to complete. During this 58 day period, 7 full query runs and a single partial run were completed. This was with queries running as close as possible to 24X7, between equipment failures and connectivity issues.

During the test the initial 2-disk SCSI array failed during the second query set run. This array failure required a database rebuild and reload on the provided ATA array. After the SCSI failure the entire initial query run had to be repeated, and compared to the SCSI results. The decision was made at that time to discard the SCSI results and continue with the ATA array.

The initial *nologging* and *noarchiving* runs performed poorly as evidenced by the test where query 1, that required 9 minutes on the SSD array, hadn't returned after 30 hours. The *nologging* and *noarchivelogging* set points were utilized during subsequent tests to allow the tests to complete in a reasonable amount of time. The *nologging* and *noarchivelogging* set points were used since turning on *logging* and *archivelog* would further stress the I/O subsystem and result in even poorer performance. The following issues further complicated the testing:

- When running the queries against the 100% SCSI/ATA database, query 1 would not complete, so after 30 hours it was halted.

- When running the queries against the 100% SCSI/ATA database, query 4 would not complete in 30 hours and it was halted.

- When running against the 100% SCSI/ATA database, query 8 produced the error codes shown below then terminated the session causing all subsequent queries to fail in run 1 and ultimately require a restart

```
Sun Jun  6 11:43:16 2004
Errors in file /home/oracle/admin/dss/udump/dss_ora_615.trc:
ORA-00600: internal error code, arguments:
[kftts2bz_many_files], [0], [39218], [], [], [], [], []
Sun Jun  6 11:43:17 2004
Errors in file /home/oracle/admin/dss/udump/dss_ora_615.trc:
ORA-07445: exception encountered: core dump [kghbigasp()+289]
[SIGSEGV] [Address not mapped to object] [0x427A8] [] []
ORA-00600: internal error code, arguments:
[kftts2bz_many_files], [0], [39218], [], [], [], [], []
Sun Jun  6 11:43:18 2004
Errors in file /home/oracle/admin/dss/udump/dss_ora_615.trc:
ORA-07445: exception encountered: core dump [kghbigasp()+289]
[SIGSEGV] [Address not mapped to object] [0x427A8] [] []
ORA-07445: exception encountered: core dump [kghbigasp()+289]
[SIGSEGV] [Address not mapped to object] [0x427A8] [] []
ORA-00600: internal error code, arguments:
[kftts2bz_many_files], [0], [39218], [], [], [], [], []
Sun Jun  6 11:43:18 2004
```

```
Errors in file /home/oracle/admin/dss/udump/dss_ora_615.trc:
ORA-07445: exception encountered: core dump [kghbigasp()+289]
[SIGSEGV] [Address not mapped to object] [0x427A8] [] []
ORA-07445: exception encountered: core dump [kghbigasp()+289]
[SIGSEGV] [Address not mapped to object] [0x427A8] [] []
ORA-07445: exception encountered: core dump [kghbigasp()+289]
[SIGSEGV] [Address not mapped to object] [0x427A8] [] []
ORA-00600: internal error code, arguments:
[kftts2bz_many_files], [0], [39218], [], [], [], [], []
[oracle@AMD43 bdump]$
[oracle@AMD43 bdump]$ tail -f alert_dss.log
Errors in file /home/oracle/admin/dss/udump/dss_ora_615.trc:
ORA-07445: exception encountered: core dump [kghbigasp()+289]
[SIGSEGV] [Address not mapped to object] [0x427A8] [] []
ORA-07445: exception encountered: core dump [kghbigasp()+289]
[SIGSEGV] [Address not mapped to object] [0x427A8] [] []
ORA-00600: internal error code, arguments:
[kftts2bz_many_files], [0], [39218], [], [], [], [], []
Sun Jun  6 11:43:18 2004
Errors in file /home/oracle/admin/dss/udump/dss_ora_615.trc:
ORA-07445: exception encountered: core dump [kghbigasp()+289]
[SIGSEGV] [Address not mapped to object] [0x427A8] [] []
ORA-07445: exception encountered: core dump [kghbigasp()+289]
[SIGSEGV] [Address not mapped to object] [0x427A8] [] []
ORA-07445: exception encountered: core dump [kghbigasp()+289]
[SIGSEGV] [Address not mapped to object] [0x427A8] [] []
ORA-00600: internal error code, arguments:
[kftts2bz_many_files], [0], [39218], [], [], [], [], []
```

- The queries would run out of temporary and undo segment space and generate the above errors if run back-to-back with the same user information. The same settings for tablespace size and relative placement were used as in the SSD runs. The script running the queries was modified to include a new connect statement before each query, releasing previous undo segments and temp segments for reuse. This was not required in the SSD tests since each run was actually several smaller runs restarted at the point of failure.

- During run 2 of the initial SCSI test, the array failed after approximately 8 days of 24X7 processing. This required a rebuild of the database on the new ATA array.

- During the final runs, 2 days of downtime were encountered as a result of a complete power outage that caused a re-assignment of the ATA array address. The data was fully recovered through the automated recovery process and the testing resumed.

- Several days were also lost due to connectivity issues.

- Any query that required longer than ~30 hours was terminated and processing restarted at the next query in the file. This was required on queries 1, 3, 13, 13a, 17, 18 in various configurations. The resulting time was set to 1440 minutes (24 hours) for these queries and the graph axis set to logarithmic to allow Figure 4.2 to show at least some of the shorter query times.

Once the initial issues with the SCSI and then ATA performance were worked out, testing was able to resume on the ATA array. Here are the configurations that were tested.

ATA Configurations

Given the timing issues already present in the ATA testing environment, the decision was made to not switch to archive log mode and table and index level logging for the test runs. In addition, the query stream was modified to allow reconnection of the test user between runs to force release of the undo and temporary segments. Why this was required in the ATA testing and not in the SSD testing is unclear but it is probably due to the excessive time required to run most of the ATA queries.

The ATA array was tested for the following configurations:

- Nologging and noarchive base run

- Nologging and noarchive

- Logs and temp files on SSD

- Data on SSD full buffer memory (1 gigabyte)

- Data on SSD half buffer memory (500 megabytes)

The results for the queries are shown in Figure 4.2. The percentage difference between SSD and SATA is so large it is not feasible to report them. However, the total elapsed times, adding in a base of 1440 minutes per each non-complete query for the SCSI, show a factor of 179 times difference between the SSD and ATA results in favor of the SSD drives. Remember that the queries for the SSD tests all completed, while several in the ATA tests were halted at the 24 hour point.

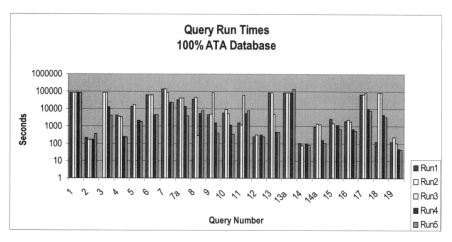

Figure 4.2: *ATA Run Times*

Please note that in order to plot the results on a single plot the vertical scale had to be switched to logarithmic. Therefore the changes in query time may only appear to be slight on the graph but may actually be several tens of percentage points. Review the detailed results in Appendix D. The runs not involving the SSD showed consistent results.

When the temp and undo tablespaces were moved to the SSD drives some queries improved while others got worse. When the data tablespace was moved to SSD all query times were improved by an average of 100 percent.

The reduction of *db_cache_size* by half with the data tablespace on SSD actually shows some improvements in performance on queries 2, 8, 11, 13, 13a while the others performed worse than the full memory levels. However all of the queries performed better with the data on the SSD than the ones on 100% ATA.

Needless to say, concerns about SSD performance were laid firmly and completely to rest when the first query on the SCSI and ATA tests had to be aborted at the 30 hour+ point. While at least a 30% improvement in query speeds was expected based on the previous insert and update based tests, it was a very pleasant surprise when the factor of 176 times improvement for overall query time was revealed.

Next it is time to compare the various SSD and ATA test scenarios.

Comparing the Different Scenarios

The main focus for testing was determining the raw performance of SSD verses disk technology. The following is a list of the scenarios tested:

- SSD performance with the DSS type queries with no logging and no archive logging

- SSD Performance with the DSS type queries with logging and archive logging

- Regular Disk Performance for DSS type queries with no logging and no archive logging

- Regular Disk performance for DSS type queries with NL and NAL and temporary and undo segments on SSD

- Regular disk performance for DSS type queries with NL and NAL and data on the SSD

- Regular disk performance for DSS type queries with NL and NAL and memory reduced.

The SSD scenarios will be examined first to determine what conclusions can be reached.

SSD Scenario Comparisons

Overall SSD performance was uniform with the exception of the initial run when memory areas used in later queries where being loaded. Assuming that the data loaded and then read from Oracle memory structures was nearly identical for each set of identical queries with identical initialization parameters, the SSD outperformed the regular disks for DSS queries by at least two orders of magnitude.

In comparing the total time for all queries to complete, the SSD database out performed the normal disk databases by a minimum factor of 179. Recall that several of the normal disk queries had to be halted at the 24 hour point in order to be able to complete the query runs in a reasonable amount of time. Therefore the true magnitude of the difference in times between the SSD and normal disk runs is technically much higher. Table 4.1 (above) lists the results form the 7 SSD runs.

Disregarding runs that followed a database restart, the performances across the various scenarios were within a couple of percent of each other. Runs 1 and 7 both followed restarts and also showed comparable results. Documented research exists that indicates that these results will hold even with multi-user access. The reason being that no disk latency, read blocking, or other disk access issues are encountered with SSD technology. In fact, until the I/O channels get flooded, all users should experience similar performance. With proper configuration, transfer rates of up to 2 gigabytes per second are possible using SSD technology.

While some queries required up to 10 minutes to achieve results on the SSD array, this was still substantially less time than the same queries required on either the SCSI or ATA arrays. Since some of the SCSI and ATA queries never finished within the boundaries of our test configurations, it is not possible to know how long they would have taken. Now the SCSI and ATA scenarios will be examined.

SCSI/ATA Scenario Comparisons

Recall that the testing architecture utilized consisted of both a SCSI array and an ATA array. The SCSI array consisted of two striped 15K RPM 36 Gigabyte Cheetah SCSI disks with a strip width of 128K, which is a standard stripe width used in many Oracle installations. And when that array failed, a 7 disk ATA array of 7200 RPM 200 gigabyte ATA drives striped at 64K.

Due to the failure of the SCSI array, its initial results were compared to the initial ATA results. Since the difference for query performance was less than 5%, the SCSI results were discarded and the ATA results used for the tests.

In the SCSI/ATA query runs there was more diversity in the results as evidence by the data in Table 4.2.

SCSI/ATA QUERY	RUN1	RUN2	RUN3	RUN4	RUN5
1	86400.00	86400.00	86400.00	86400.00	86400.00
2	207.62	161.84	162.90	165.08	358.03
3	0.00	86400.00	86400.00	12657.46	4317.06
4	4313.82	3666.76	3372.94	243.31	228.24
5	13568.08	17804.46	0.00	2145.11	1912.33
6	61926.08	61367.15	61547.58	4823.09	4581.85
7	133456.46	132743.60	86400.00	23259.28	22497.74
7a	33038.67	40758.41	41817.98	13807.28	4158.16
8	36062.61	46331.87	284.91	5361.54	8134.71
9	4779.68	5138.53	86400.00	1550.05	406.09
10	6125.83	9278.53	5544.37	1164.96	347.61
11	1650.96	1144.37	62632.58	5602.72	8191.45
12	249.64	319.86	0.00	300.85	256.31
13	86400.00	86400.00	5283.60	444.54	457.22
13a	86400.00	86400.00	86400.00	86400.00	131326.99
14	106.79	75.49	0.00	94.00	86.51
14a	917.28	1323.80	1228.10	154.44	108.91
15	2803.80	1511.22	0.00	1205.10	690.55
16	1958.00	2309.16	1909.33	662.30	519.49
17	65826.95	66631.73	86400.00	10388.28	7947.97
18	118.65	86400.00	86400.00	4597.52	3471.07
19	120.06	222.30	108.98	49.91	46.28
Total Sec	626430.98	822789.08	788693.27	261476.82	286444.57
Total Days	7.25	9.52	9.13	3.03	3.32

Table 4.2: *Raw Data from the ATA Query Runs*

Given that the reads were spread over 7 disks in the ATA array which provided an effective possible read profile of nearly a thousand or more I/O's/sec and assuming an I/O of at least one stripe width would translate into 64 megabyte to 128 megabyte I/O's per second. 64k is standard I/O for most UNIX environments with a maximum physical I/O possible of roughly 1 megabyte. From the *env* dump, the Linux system was set at the default of 128K maximum physical I/O.

The ATA array was expected to perform much better than it did in these tests. Here is a look at the SCSI/ATA results.

Standard SCSI/ATA Runs

Runs 1 and 2 were standard query runs with the exception that they were performed using *nologging* and *no archivelog* mode. With notable differences, in most cases run 1 query times were longer than run 2 times due to the increased need for disk reads to populate the data cache in the Oracle memory system. Table 4.2 shows that several queries weren't able to run to completion and overall performance was poor.

Run 3 with Temporary and Undo on SSD

Run 3 placed the temporary and undo segments on the SSD array. This improved the response time for queries that used many sorts or hash joins such as 8, 10 and 13. This allowed 13 to finish in less than 24 hours. But overall, the gains did not outweigh the losses. For this size database the hash and sort activity was able to complete within the 2 gigabytes allowed for the *pga_max_allocation* set point. Moving the temporary tablespace to SSD was not a big factor in performance. Since nologging was used while performing query activity, the undo requirements were minimal. Consequently, moving the undo segments also had little effect on performance. However, in databases where there were more temporary and undo related waits, this would play more of a factor in query performance.

Run 4 with DATA on SSD

In run 4 the data segments were moved to the SSD and the temporary and undo segments were placed back on normal drives. While taking into consideration the two queries that could not complete, the total run time still improved by a factor of 3. And in many cases the run times even improved by a factor of 10.

Dramatic improvement is to be expected considering the large number of scattered and sequential read waits experienced by the instance. While moving the data files to the SSD arrays may not affect the number of such waits, it dramatically affects the duration of each wait.

Run 5 with Data on SSD and Reduced Memory

In an effort to gauge the importance of setting *db_cache_size* when using SSD assets, in run 5 the *db_cache_size* was reduced by 50% from 1 gigabyte to 500 megabytes. The results were surprising in that the overall run time was reduced by 8 percent with most queries showing some improvement in runtime. However, this may be affected by several queries that didn't complete before having completed run 4 and populating the smaller cache with useful data. This would be one area of additional research for future work.

Conclusion

In the SSD verses ATA benchmark the gains for insert and update processing as shown in the database loading and index build scenarios was a respectable 30%. This 30% was due to the CPU overhead involved in the insert and update activities. If the Oracle level processing for insert and update activities could be optimized for SSD, significant performance gains might be realized during these activities.

The most significant performance gain comes in the use of SSD in query based transaction loads. The performance gains for using SSD can be quite spectacular, factors of 176 times better performance over standard disk technologies are documented in this chapter.

In this chapter, Oracle performance with queries on SSD and ATA technology arrays has been covered. The results and potential benefits of the effects of moving various types of files to the SSD array has been demonstrated

Even when only data files can be placed on SSD assets, the performance gains are phenomenal, possibly up to or greater than 300%, as also shown in the benchmarks.

Proper use of SSD assets can make a significant improvement in performance. Determining if or how user systems can benefit from SSD technology is the topic for the next chapter.

Is SSD Right for Your Database?

Introduction

In previous chapters the actual results form the comparison of SSD to SCSI and ATA technologies has been examined. However, is SSD technology the right choice for all Oracle databases? At least for the near term, SSD technology is not an inexpensive option. How is the best way to determine if adding it to the technology infrastructure will improve performance? Covered in this chapter are some guidelines and analysis techniques to determine if SSD technology is the right choice.

When is SSD right for you?

Analyzing What to Put On SSD

Now that it has been demonstrated that SSD technology can be a great help to certain types of systems, how does a DBA determine if internal implementation is warranted? This chapter will provide insight into the methods used to analyze a system to see if SSD technology will help.

The choices of what to put on the SSD drive breakdown into several general areas:

- Data
- Indexes
- Redo logs
- Temporary files

It is more critical to place the above files than it is files such as control files and archive logs since they do not generally cause performance issues. Here are some analysis tools to determine what files should be placed on SSD arrays.

Carefully investigate your test results!

Analysis Tools

Analysis to determine what to place on SSD files falls under two categories, operating system level analysis and Oracle internal analysis. Both methods involve analyzing the I/O wait interface from either the system or Oracle perspective. In many situations the operating system level analysis may be inconclusive due to the combining of physical disks into large, RAID combined logical disks. In this case, look at the I/O to the individual datafiles from the Oracle perspective.

Inside Oracle there are two areas to look at to determine the best candidates for placement on the SSD asset. These two are the I/O statistics and the wait interface statistics. Looking at the I/O interface for average I/O times and total I/O to specific datafiles help determine usage patterns for datafiles and temp files. Looking at the wait interface helps determine if processes are waiting on I/O related events and what events are being waited on. There are several possible sources for the I/O and wait interface statistics:

- Custom scripts
- Oracle Enterprise Manager
- Third-Party tools
- STATSPACK reports

The use of custom scripts gives the analyst control over the selection and display of specific statistics of concern. Oracle Enterprise manager provides a plethora of data, but may not be available at all sites. Third-party tools also provide a wealth of data but are expensive and may not be installed at all client sites. STATSPACK reports are available at all sites, provide a wealth of statistics, and allow a focused look at specific time intervals. Of the available data gathering methods, scripts and STATSPACK will be the focus of this chapter. Custom scripts will be reviewed first for their use in determining the effectiveness of SSD technology conversion.

Custom Scripts

Generally speaking, custom scripts utilize the *v$* series of views to generate reports showing I/O distribution, timing data, and wait statistics. For data and temp file related statistics the *v$filestat* and *v$tempstat* tables are utilized. For wait interface information the *v$waitstat, v$sysstat* and *v$sesstat* tables can be utilized. Here is a sample script for generating I/O related data.

🖫   **Example Script to Generate I/O Statistics**

```
--   ****************************************************
-- Copyright © 2003 by Rampant TechPress
-- This script is free for non-commercial purposes
-- with no warranties.  Use at your own risk.
--
-- To license this script for a commercial purpose,
-- contact info@rampant.cc
```

```
--  ***************************************************
column sum_io1 new_value st1 noprint
column sum_io2 new_value st2 noprint
column sum_io new_value divide_by noprint
column Percent format 999.999 heading 'Percent|Of IO'
column brratio format 999.99 heading 'Block|Read|Ratio'
column bwratio format 999.99 heading 'Block|Write|Ratio'
column phyrds heading 'Phys|Reads'
column phywrts heading 'Phys|Writes'
column phyblkrd heading 'Phys|Block|Reads'
column phyblkwrt heading 'Phys|Block|Writes'
column name format a45 heading 'File|Name'
column file# format 9999 heading 'File'
set feedback off verify off lines 132 pages 60 sqlbl on trims on
rem
select
    nvl(sum(a.phyrds+a.phywrts),0) sum_io1
from
    sys.v_$filestat a;
select nvl(sum(b.phyrds+b.phywrts),0) sum_io2
from
      sys.v_$tempstat b;
select &st1+&st2 sum_io from dual;
rem
ttitle 'File I/O Statistics Report'
spool fileio
select
    a.file#,b.name, a.phyrds, a.phywrts,
    (100*(a.phyrds+a.phywrts)/&divide_by) Percent,
    a.phyblkrd, a.phyblkwrt, (a.phyblkrd/greatest(a.phyrds,1))
brratio,
      (a.phyblkwrt/greatest(a.phywrts,1)) bwratio
from
    sys.v_$filestat a, sys.v_$dbfile b
where
    a.file#=b.file#
union
select
    c.file#,d.name, c.phyrds, c.phywrts,
    (100*(c.phyrds+c.phywrts)/&divide_by) Percent,
    c.phyblkrd, c.phyblkwrt,(c.phyblkrd/greatest(c.phyrds,1))
brratio,
      (c.phyblkwrt/greatest(c.phywrts,1)) bwratio
from
    sys.v_$tempstat c, sys.v_$tempfile d
where
    c.file#=d.file#
order by 1;
spool off
pause Press enter to continue
set feedback on verify on lines 80 pages 22
clear columns
ttitle off
```

Note that both the *v$filestat* and *v$tempstat* tables are utilized and the results are compared to a total I/O figure so each datafile and tempfiles I/O is captured. Also recall that the *v$* views, and the *gv$* views in RAC, contain cumulative statistics beginning when the database started.

For Oracle RAC environments, the *gv$* version of these tables needs to be utilized so that total I/O across all instances is captured since the *v$* views only capture statistics for the single instance. Here is an example of the output for our environment with ATA drives.

```
Mon Jul 19                                                              page    1
                           File I/O Statistics Report
                                                        Phys   Phys Block Block
         File                        Phys   Phys Percent Block  Block Read  Write
File Name                           Reads Writes of I/O Reads Writes Ratio Ratio
---- ------------------------------- -------- ------ ------- -------- ------ ----- -----
   1 /u08/oracle/oradata/dss/system01.dbf    12857   1201   .015    47975   1201  3.73  1.00
   1 /u12/oracle/oradata/dss/tem101.dbf       8733  25480   .036    80127 338717  9.18 13.29
   2 /u09/oracle/oradata/dss/undotbs101.dbf     50   2979   .003       50   2979  1.00  1.00
   2 /u12/oracle/oradata/dss/tem102.dbf          4      0   .000        4      0  1.00   .00
   3 /u12/oracle/oradata/dss/temp05.dbf          4      0   .000        4      0  1.00   .00
   3 /u12/oracle/oradata/dss/undotbs103.dbf     50    397   .000       50    397  1.00  1.00
   4 /u01/oracle/oradata/dss/temp021.dbf         0      0   .000        0      0   .00   .00
   4 /u12/oracle/oradata/dss/undotbs102.dbf    313   3157   .004      313   3157  1.00  1.00
   5 /u02/oracle/oradata/dss/temp022.dbf         0      0   .000        0      0   .00   .00
   5 /u08/oracle/oradata/dss/dss_data01.dbf 33688717      3 35.631 34889652      3  1.04  1.00
   6 /u09/oracle/oradata/dss/dss_data02.dbf 29910924      3 31.635 31075321      3  1.04  1.00
   7 /u10/oracle/oradata/dss/dss_data03.dbf 30345274      3 32.095 31504507      3  1.04  1.00
   8 /u11/oracle/oradata/dss/dss_index01.dbf  182678      3   .193   243693      3  1.33  1.00
   9 /u13/oracle/oradata/dss/dss_index02.dbf  181979      3   .192   245391      3  1.35  1.00
  10 /u14/oracle/oradata/dss/dss_index03.dbf  173160      3   .183   233697      3  1.35  1.00
  11 /u09/oracle/oradata/dss/drsys01.dbf          5      3   .000        5      3  1.00  1.00
  12 /u09/oracle/oradata/dss/tools01.dbf          5      3   .000        5      3  1.00  1.00
  13 /u10/oracle/oradata/dss/xdb01.dbf           11      3   .000       23      3  2.09  1.00
  14 /u13/oracle/oradata/dss/dss_index3.dbf   11554      3   .012    11554      3  1.00  1.00
  15 /u10/oracle/oradata/dss/dss_index05.dbf      5      3   .000        5      3  1.00  1.00
  16 /u09/oracle/oradata/dss/dss_index06.dbf      5      3   .000        5      3  1.00  1.00
  17 /u08/oracle/oradata/dss/dss_index07.dbf      5      3   .000        5      3  1.00  1.00
  18 /u03/oracle/oradata/dss/undo021.dbf          0      3   .000        0      3   .00  1.00
  19 /u04/oracle/oradata/dss/uno022.dbf           0      3   .000        0      3   .00  1.00
```

Note that 98% of the I/O is being directed to the *dss_data* tablespace datafiles with the *dss_index* datafiles having .580% and temporary tablespace having .036 percent. This report indicates that the major stress is being placed on the data datafiles.

A look at the operating system *iostat* command confirms that the I/O subsystem is undergoing an extreme amount of stress. The results of an *iostat* command are shown below with the averages since system startup being omitted.

```
avg-cpu:  %user   %nice    %sys   %idle
           0.20    0.00    0.60   99.20

Device:           tps  Blk_read/s  Blk_wrtn/s  Blk_read  Blk_wrtn
dev3-0          59.04      854.62      269.88      2128       672
dev8-0           0.00        0.00        0.00         0         0
dev8-1        1795.18    14361.45        0.00     35760         0

avg-cpu:  %user   %nice    %sys   %idle
           0.40    0.00    1.39   98.21

Device:           tps  Blk_read/s  Blk_wrtn/s  Blk_read  Blk_wrtn
dev3-0          55.16      736.51       60.32      1856       152
dev8-0           0.00        0.00        0.00         0         0
dev8-1        1796.03    14374.60        0.00     36224         0
```

Note that device 8-1, the ATA drive array, is doing the majority of the work in the system. CPU time is registering as 98% idle which might lead one to think that the system was idling along, not seeing much stress. However, a look at the top command shows the error in this assumption. The output of the top command for the same time period is shown here.

```
21:01:35  up 14 days,  3:32,  1 user,  load average: 2.00, 2.00, 2.00
65 processes: 64 sleeping, 1 running, 0 zombie, 0 stopped
CPU states:  cpu     user    nice   system      irq  softirq   iowait      idle
            total     0.4%    0.0%     0.0%     0.4%     0.0%    49.5%     49.5%
            cpu00     0.0%    0.0%     0.0%     0.9%     0.0%     0.0%     99.0%
            cpu01     0.9%    0.0%     0.0%     0.0%     0.0%    99.0%      0.0%
Mem:  4067556k av, 4048420k used,   19136k free,       0k shrd,  281432k buff
                   3063424k actv,  798872k in_d,   20108k in_c
Swap: 2040244k av,  577540k used, 1462704k free   3555660k cached
```

This was just the header from an I/O stat taken during the ATA query runs. The CPU is showing 98% idle because the processor handling the I/O for the query is 100% bound. This is also confirmed by the *vmstat* command. The results of which are shown below:

```
procs                      memory      swap          io     system         cpu
 r  b   swpd   free   buff  cache   si   so    bi    bo   in   cs us sy id wa
 1  1 574436  18864 281432 3557252   13    1    17     7   16    2  3  2  1  6
 0  2 575580  18688 281432 3557580  142   61  3770    82  628  811  1  4 46 49
 1  2 575164  18736 281432 3557728  167  311  3808   337  638  843  0  1 50 49
 0  2 574740  19496 281432 3556400  188    0  3923    16  639  838  0  1 50 49
 1  1 577084  18724 281432 3557972  195  118  3684   142  615  797  0  1 50 50
 2  0 576552  18752 281432 3557452  223    0  3487    36  588  773  0  5 48 47
 0  2 577120  19048 281432 3557268  234   34  3763    48  621  809  0  0 49 51
 1  1 576584  18704 281432 3557072  243  430  3638   454  605  775  1  1 50 49
 0  2 576124  18772 281432 3556524  202  184  3682   210  614  795  1  1 49 49
 1  1 575896  19372 281432 3558408  169  120  3769   134  622  820  0  1 49 49
```

I/O timing data from inside Oracle is also a critical component of the analysis. The script that follows shows an example query to get the I/O timing data for the various data and temp files.

💾 Example I/O Timing Script

```
-- ************************************************
-- Copyright © 2003 by Rampant TechPress
-- This script is free for non-commercial purposes
-- with no warranties.  Use at your own risk.
--
-- To license this script for a commercial purpose,
-- contact info@rampant.cc
-- ************************************************

Col file# format 99999 heading 'File#'
col name format a45 heading 'Name'
col phywrts heading 'Phys.|Writes'
col phyrds heading 'Phys.|Reads'
col read_rat heading 'Avg.|Read|Time' format 990.000
col write_rat heading 'Avg.|Write|Time' format 990.000
set lines 132 pages 45
ttitle 'I/O Timing Analysis'
spool io_time
select  f.FILE# ,d.name,PHYRDS,PHYWRTS,READTIM/greatest(PHYRDS,1)
read_rat,WRITETIM/greatest(PHYWRTS,1) write_rat
from v$filestat f, v$datafile d
where f.file#=d.file#
union
select  f.FILE# ,d.name,PHYRDS,PHYWRTS,READTIM/greatest(PHYRDS,1)
read_rat,WRITETIM/greatest(PHYWRTS,1) write_rat
from v$tempstat f, v$tempfile d
where f.file#=d.file#
order by 5 desc;
spool off
ttitle off
clear columns
set lines 80 pages 22
```

The script queries the *v$tempfile* and *v$datafile* views for timing data and shows the average time per I/O operation on the files. Here is a sample report:

```
                                                         Avg.      Avg.
                                              Phys.  Phys.  Read    Write
File#  Name                                   Reads  Writes  Time    Time
-----  -------------------------------------  -----------  -------  -------  -------
    3  /u12/oracle/oradata/dss/undotbs103.dbf      50     397  1.400   0.073
   13  /u10/oracle/oradata/dss/xdb01.dbf           11       3  1.363   0.333
    1  /u08/oracle/oradata/dss/system01.dbf     12857    1201  1.127   0.087
    4  /u11/oracle/oradata/dss/undotbs102.dbf     313    3157  0.785   0.069
    2  /u09/oracle/oradata/dss/undotbs101.dbf      50    2979  0.760   0.064
    2  /u12/oracle/oradata/dss/tem102.dbf           4       0  0.500   0.000
    1  /u12/oracle/oradata/dss/tem101.dbf        8733   25480  0.480   0.599
    5  /u08/oracle/oradata/dss/dss_data01.dbf 33688717      3  0.448   0.000
    7  /u10/oracle/oradata/dss/dss_data03.dbf 30345274      3  0.444   0.000
    6  /u09/oracle/oradata/dss/dss_data02.dbf 29910924      3  0.441   0.000
   11  /u09/oracle/oradata/dss/drsys01.dbf          5       3  0.400   0.333
    3  /u12/oracle/oradata/dss/temp05.dbf           4       0  0.250   0.000
   12  /u09/oracle/oradata/dss/tools01.dbf          5       3  0.200   0.000
   15  /u10/oracle/oradata/dss_index05.dbf          5       3  0.200   0.000
   16  /u09/oracle/oradata/dss_index06.dbf          5       3  0.200   0.000
   17  /u08/oracle/oradata/dss_index07.dbf          5       3  0.200   0.000
   10  /u14/oracle/oradata/dss/dss_index03.dbf 173160      3  0.110   0.000
    9  /u13/oracle/oradata/dss/dss_index02.dbf 181979      3  0.106   0.000
    8  /u11/oracle/oradata/dss/dss_index01.dbf 182678      3  0.102   0.333
   14  /u13/oracle/oradata/dss/dss_index3.dbf   11554      3  0.017   0.000
    4  /u01/oracle/oradata/dss/temp021.dbf          0       0  0.000   0.000
    5  /u02/oracle/oradata/dss/temp022.dbf          0       0  0.000   0.000
   18  /u03/oracle/oradata/dss/undo021.dbf          0       3  0.000   0.000
   19  /u04/oracle/oradata/dss/uno022.dbf           0       3  0.000   0.000

24 rows selected.
```

The I/O times are actually quite acceptable for a disk I/O subsystem. All I/O times for the filesystems of concern are fractional milliseconds. However, when the volume of I/O operations is large, even a fractional time multiples rapidly and moving to SSD assets is indicated.

To review what has been covered so far is the use of scripts to determine I/O rates and timings. From this data one can determine which files are experiencing the most I/O and are candidates for placement on the SSD drive. However, this is not the total picture, the wait interface should be examined to see if the I/O is actually generating wait related issues.

Don't panic if test results don't match expectations!

While self generated scripts can be used, the Oracle provided STATSPACK scripts do a great job on reporting against the wait interface.

Using the STATSPACK Report to Analyze I/O Performance

The STATSPACK utility is shipped with every Oracle Database since version 8.1.7.2. The commonality makes it a logical choice for analyzing databases for use with SSD. STATSPACK provides a plethora of I/O related statistics as well as all the needed wait interface statistics.

Installing STATSPACK

Installation of STATSPACK is actually quite simple:

1. Create a tablespace in which to store the captured STATSPACK statistics. Usually 100-500 megabytes is sufficient, however use 500m if using STATSPACK on a continuing basis. This is called PERFSTAT.

2. From the SYS user run the STATSPACK user, table and packaged creation script. This is typically:

```
$ORACLE_HOME/rdbms/admin/spcreate.sql
```

   Be aware that this may be different on older Oracle releases.

3. Log in as the perfstat user, and execute the STATSPACK.snap procedure.

4. Wait for a reasonable collection interval, then re-run the STATSPACK.snap procedure.

5. For the internal from which data was just collected and from the perfstat user, run the STATSPACK reporting script:

```
$ORACLE_HOME/rdbms/admin/spreport
```

Now that STATSPACK is installed, the system can be analyzed to see if SSD technology is appropriate. Here is a review of a few STATSPACK results from the benchmark test runs and some examples taken from actual operating systems to see if SSD technology can help.

Impartial reviews of your results add credibility!

Reviewing the STATSPACK Report for SSD

The STATSPACK report can run to dozens of pages depending on the number of files, amount of SQL generated, and a number of other parameters. However, in determining what files should be placed on SSD assets the most important section of the report is the one dealing with the wait interface. On the first page of the report the top five wait events are shown. Listed below is the STATSPACK report for a run with the data files on the ATA drives.

```
Top 5 Timed Events
~~~~~~~~~~~~~~~~~~                                           % Total
Event                                  Waits    Time (s) Ela Time
------------------------------------ ------------ ----------- --------
db file sequential read              93,211,687    398,236    96.80
CPU time                                            10,892     2.65
db file scattered read                  344,252      1,512      .37
control file parallel write             141,759        583      .14
latch free                                8,947         90      .02
                                     ------------ ----------- --------
```

For those not familiar with the various waits captured by the wait interface, Table 5.1 shows the major I/O related waits.

EVENT	WAIT	DESCRIPTION
Datafile I/O-Related Wait Events:		
sequential read	db file	Wait for single block read of a table or index
scattered read	db file	Wait for Multi-block read of a table or index (full scan)
parallel read	db file	Used when Oracle performs in parallel reads from multiple datafiles to non-contiguous buffers in memory (PGA or Buffer Cache). Similar to db file sequential read
path read	direct	Used by Oracle when reading directly into PGA (sort or hash)
path write	direct	Used by Oracle when writing directly into PGA (sort or hash)
path read (lob)	direct	Read of a LOB segment
path write (lob)	direct	Write of a LOB segment
Controlfile I/O-Related Wait Events:		
file parallel write	control	Waiting for the writes of CF records to the CF files
file sequential read	control	Occurs on I/O to a single copy of the controlfile
file single write	control	Occurs on I/O to a single copy of the controlfile
Redo Logging I/O-Related Wait Events:		
parallel write	log file	Waiting for the writes of redo records to the redo log files
sync	log file	User session waits on this wait event while waiting for LGWR to post after commit write of dirty blocks

WAIT EVENT	DESCRIPTION
log file sequential read	LGWR background process waits for this event while it is copying redo records from the memory Log Buffer cache to the current redo group's member logfiles on disk.
log file single write	This Wait Event is I/O-related so it is likely to appear together with 'log file parallel write'
switch logfile command	Wait cause by manual redo log switch command
log file switch completion	Wait generated while buffers are written during log switch
log file switch (clearing log file)	Wait generated while buffers are written during log switch
log file switch (checkpoint incomplete)	Wait generated while buffers are written during log switch when checkpoint takes longer than normal
log switch/archive	Wait generated while buffers are written during log switch
log file switch (archiving needed)	Wait generated while buffers are written during log switch when write cannot be achieved immediately to archive log location

Table 5.1: *I/O Related Wait Events*

In the previously listed STATSPACK report for a run with the data files on the ATA drives the db file sequential read wait event dominated the events display. Referring to Table 5.1 this is due to single block reads of indexes or tables. With nearly 97% of non-idle wait time this is clearly what needs to be examined.

The following listing shows the results from a STATSPACK taken with the data files on the SSD drives. If only the data files are moved to the SSD asset there is a 93% drop in I/O related wait time from 398,236 to 31,030 for the same queries even though actual waits remained virtually unchanged, 93,211,687 versus 99,991,232. Notice that CPU time has also dropped to 30% of its previous value.

```
Top 5 Timed Events
~~~~~~~~~~~~~~~~~~                                          % Total
Event                                      Waits   Time (s) Ela Time
-------------------------------------- ------------ ----------- --------
db file sequential read                  99,991,232    31,030    88.65
CPU time                                                3,343     9.55
control file parallel write                  19,300       375     1.07
db file scattered read                      174,949       157      .45
control file sequential read                  7,764        50      .14
                                       ------------------------------------------------
```

Another section of the STATSPACK report which must be utilized for determining I/O characteristics is the data file I/O section. The following is the I/O section of the STATSPACK report for the run with the data files on the ATA drives.

Tablespace				Filename				
Reads	Av Reads/s	Av Rd(ms)	Av Blks/Rd	Writes	Av Writes/s	Buffer Waits	Av Buf Wt(ms)	
DSS_DATA				/u08/oracle/oradata/dss/dss_data01.dbf				
33,299,194	76	4.4	1.1	0	0	0		
				/u09/oracle/oradata/dss/dss_data02.dbf				
29,693,254	68	4.3	1.1	0	0	0		
				/u10/oracle/oradata/dss/dss_data03.dbf				
30,079,180	69	4.4	1.1	0	0	0		
DSS_INDEX				/u11/oracle/oradata/dss/dss_index01.dbf				
159,622	0	6.2	1.0	0	0	0		
				/u13/oracle/oradata/dss/dss_index02.dbf				
151,677	0	7.2	1.0	0	0	0		
				/u13/oracle/oradata/dss/dss_index3.dbf				
11,549	0	0.1	1.0	0	0	0		
				/u14/oracle/oradata/dss/dss_index03.dbf				
149,736	0	7.3	1.0	0	0	0		
PERFSTAT				/u05/oracle/oradata/dss/perfstat1.dbf				
10	0	2.0	1.5	172	0	0		
SYSTEM				/u08/oracle/oradata/dss/system01.dbf				
11,375	0	12.6	4.0	998	0	0		
TEMP2				/u01/oracle/oradata/dss/temp021.dbf				
138,030	0	0.3	3.4	46,979	0	0		
				/u02/oracle/oradata/dss/temp022.dbf				
139,933	0	0.2	2.3	33,505	0	0		
UNDO2				/u03/oracle/oradata/dss/undo021.dbf				
56	0	4.5	1.0	4,162	0	17	30.6	
				/u04/oracle/oradata/dss/uno022.dbf				
116	0	2.6	1.0	1,241	0	0		

The previous report shows that the data files are experiencing the majority of the I/O stress with the most I/O's/second and high read times. The following report shows that once the data files are moved to the SSD drive these values change dramatically.

```
File I/O Stats for DB: DSS   Instance: dss   Snaps: 1 -2
->ordered by Tablespace, File
```

Tablespace			Filename				
Reads	Av Reads/s	Av Rd(ms)	Av Blks/Rd	Writes	Av Writes/s	Buffer Waits	Av Buf Wt(ms)
DSS_DATA			/u01/oracle/oradata/dss/dss_data01.dbf				
35,975,161	602	0.3	1.0	0	0	0	
			/u02/oracle/oradata/dss/dss_data02.dbf				
31,756,793	532	0.3	1.0	0	0	0	
			/u03/oracle/oradata/dss/dss_data03.dbf				
32,279,053	540	0.3	1.0	0	0	0	
DSS_INDEX			/u11/oracle/oradata/dss/dss_index01.dbf				
46,863	1	0.3	1.0	0	0	0	
			/u13/oracle/oradata/dss/dss_index02.dbf				
50,032	1	0.3	1.0	0	0	0	
			/u14/oracle/oradata/dss/dss_index03.dbf				
49,166	1	0.3	1.0	0	0	0	
PERFSTAT			/u12/oracle/oradata/dss/perfstat.dbf				
37	0	18.6	1.0	92	0	0	
SYSTEM			/u08/oracle/oradata/dss/system01.dbf				
5,358	0	4.3	2.0	1,549	0	0	
TEMP			/u12/oracle/oradata/dss/temp011.dbf				
113,460	2	4.5	2.7	35,450	1	0	
UNDOTBS			/u08/oracle/oradata/dss/undo01.dbf				
1,626	0	2.7	1.0	2,138	0	1	60.0
			/u09/oracle/oradata/dss/undo02.dbf				
537	0	3.4	1.0	631	0	0	

Notice how I/O per second has increased by a factor of 5-6 times while average read time has dropped from 4-5 milliseconds to 0.3 milliseconds. This difference is reflected in the query times reported earlier for runs 5 and 6.

Based on this analysis, moving the data and index tablespaces would give the best results since, based on I/O readings and on the waits, the highest stress is on the data and index datafiles Recall that *df_file_scattered_reads* are full table or full index scans, *db_file_sequential_reads* are single point reads of tables or indexes. In tests where the undo and temporary tablespaces where moved to the SSD array for this database, there were no appreciable gains in performance. Refer to ATA runs 3 and 4. However, if the majority of the waits shown were due to undo segments or temporary tablespace related activity, sort and hash related waits or direct I/O related waits for example, then moving them to the SSD asset would make sense. An important fact to remember regarding moving files to the SSD asset is that performance gains will only be realized related to the percentage of time spent waiting on that asset. If the amount of time waited on for a temporary tablespace is less than 1 percent of the total application wait time, then moving the temporary tablespace to the SSD will only realize a gain of 1 percent in performance. If the majority of the physical I/O in the system was being directed at data tablespace datafiles and causing a significant amount of wait time, then moving the data tablespace datafiles would realize significant gains in performance. If there was sufficient room on the SSD asset, moving the index tablespace data files would be the next logical choice.

Here is the timing related part of the header from another system's STATSPACK report.

```
            Snap Id    Snap Time       Sessions Curs/Sess Comment
            -------  ------------------ -------- --------- ----------
---------
Begin Snap:    11 27-Oct-03 12:00:05      19      3.4
  End Snap:    19 27-Oct-03 20:00:03      14      3.3
   Elapsed:              479.97 (mins)
```

The time span is long enough to guarantee a good sample. Ensure that the STATSPACK used is not just for a specific transaction, but covers a period of "normal" activity in the database. Here is the resulting wait profile.

```
Top 5 Timed Events
~~~~~~~~~~~~~~~~~~                                           % Total
Event                                                    Waits Ela Time
------------------------------------------------ ------------ --------
control file parallel write                             9,306    30.15
db file scattered read                                 34,516    19.27
db file sequential read                                86,156    18.18
SQL*Net message from dblink                            15,882    13.99
CPU time                                                         12.42
                                                 ------------
```

Notice how I/O related waits dominate. Oddly enough it is control file parallel writes that are the predominant wait activity. This is likely due to control files being collocated with the other database files. Logic would seem to indicate that moving the control files to SSD assets would be the appropriate course of action. However, control files are usually low I/O files and if they were moved to another disk asset their wait contribution would probably disappear.

Therefore what remains is data and index related I/O and the need to review the I/O profile for the database. Listed below is an excerpt from the I/O section of the STATSPACK report showing all datafiles with I/O greater than 500.

```
File I/O Stats for DB: TSTPROD  Instance: TSTprod  Snaps: 11 -19
->ordered by Tablespace, File

Tablespace                      Filename
--------------------            ------------------------------------------------------
                Av      Av    Av                          Av      Buffer Av Buf
         Reads Reads/s Rd(ms) Blks/Rd     Writes Writes/s   Waits Wt(ms)
------------- ------- ------ ------- ------------ -------- -------- ------
NAME_ADDRESS_JUNCTION_XI G:\ORADATA\GLOBAL_NAMES\INDEXES\NAME_ADDRESS_JUNCTIO
          502       0    6.2     1.0          218        0        0
NAME_ADDRESS_JUNCTION_XI G:\ORADATA\GLOBAL_NAMES\INDEXES\NAME_ADDRESS_JUNCTIO
          332       0    6.8     1.0          425        0        0
NAME_ADDRESS_JUNCTION_XU G:\ORADATA\GLOBAL_NAMES\INDEXES\NAME_ADDRESS_JUNCTIO
          797       0    6.3     1.0          637        0        0
NAME_ADDRESS_TBL        F:\ORADATA\GLOBAL_NAMES\TABLES\NAME_ADDRESS_TBL.DBF
          480       0    9.0     1.0          496        0        0
NAME_ADDRESS_XID        G:\ORADATA\GLOBAL_NAMES\INDEXES\NAME_ADDRESS_XID.DBF
        2,131       0    7.3     1.0        2,334        0        0
NAME_TBL                F:\ORADATA\GLOBAL_NAMES\TABLES\NAME_TBL.DBF
          489       0    7.1     1.0          189        0        0
NAME_XID                G:\ORADATA\GLOBAL_NAMES\INDEXES\NAME_XID.DBF
          574       0    8.1     1.0          733        0        0
RBS                     H:\ORADATA\GLOBAL_NAMES\RBS1.DBF
            5       0    0.0     1.0        2,198        0        0
SMALL_TBL               F:\ORADATA\GLOBAL_NAMES\TABLES\SMALL_TBL.DBF
       36,288       1    3.4    14.3           15        0       44    2.3
```

Oracle Solid State Disk Tuning

```
SYSTEM              H:\ORADATA\GLOBAL_NAMES\SYSTEM01.DBF
        75,856    3   0.8    1.0      164        0          0
TOOLS               D:\ORACLE\ORADATA\GLOBAL_NAMES\TOOLS01.DBF
          474    0   4.6    1.0    1,076        0          0
USERS               D:\ORACLE\ORADATA\GLOBAL_NAMES\USERS01.DBF
          423    0   6.1    4.8      415        0          0
XDB                 D:\ORACLE\ORADATA\GLOBAL_NAMES\XDB01.DBF
          603    0   2.9    1.0        0        0          0
```

Moving *small_tbl* or *system* would provide the biggest gain followed by moving *name_address_xid* and then *rbs*. However, in this situation I/O to *system* is excessive so the causes should be determined and eliminated.

In conclusion, the wait summary and I/O sections of the STATSPACK report provide vital clues as to whether SSD technology will help. However, make sure that the sample period is sufficiently representative of the system.

The results from the SSD runs are reviewed next.

Example STATSPACK Results from the SSD Runs

The following is the STATSPACK report for the same query and data profiles run against the SSD array instead of the SCSI/ATA arrays. This report shows the top five wait events from SSD run 5.

```
Instance Efficiency Percentages (Target 100%)
~~~~~~~~~~~~~~~~~~~~~~~~~~~~~~~~~~~~~~~~~~~~~~~~~
            Buffer Nowait %:  100.00     Redo NoWait %:  100.00
            Buffer  Hit   %:   18.83   In-memory Sort %:   99.67
            Library Hit   %:   98.72       Soft Parse %:   98.55
       Execute to Parse %:    67.94       Latch Hit %:   100.00
Parse CPU to Parse Elapsd %:  150.00     % Non-Parse CPU:  100.00

 Shared Pool Statistics         Begin   End
                                ------  ------
             Memory Usage %:    47.18   48.16
    % SQL with executions>1:    79.52   84.83
    % Memory for SQL w/exec>1:  64.58   80.39
```

```
Top 5 Timed Events
~~~~~~~~~~~~~~~~~~                                                    % Total
Event                                             Waits   Time (s) Ela Time
------------------------------------------------ ------------ ----------- --------
CPU time                                                      2,962    72.43
db file scattered read                        1,630,994       1,101    26.92
db file parallel read                             6,373          16      .39
db file sequential read                          80,346           7      .18
control file parallel write                       1,831           3      .07
                 ------------------------------------------------------------
```

Notice that the waits are still occurring for the I/O that were
seen for the SCSI and ATA runs, however now the waits are less
than the CPU processing time. The I/O profile from the run 5
report shows the majority of the I/O going against the data and
index datafiles just as was seen with the SCSI and ATA array
results. The following is the I/O profile for the SSD array from
the same STATSPACK report as shown above.

```
File I/O Stats for DB: DSS   Instance: dss   Snaps: 1 -2
->ordered by Tablespace, File

Tablespace                     Filename
----------------------         ---------------------------------------------------
              Av      Av    Av                     Av          Buffer Av Buf
       Reads Reads/s Rd(ms) Blks/Rd    Writes Writes/s   Waits Wt(ms)
------------- ------- ------ ------- ------------ -------- ---------- ------
DSS_DATA                       /u01/oracle/oradata/dss/dss_data01.dbf
     648,400     115    0.6    11.4         0        0         0
                               /u02/oracle/oradata/dss/dss_data02.dbf
     571,656     102    0.6    11.5         0        0         0
                               /u03/oracle/oradata/dss/dss_data03.dbf
     581,510     103    0.6    11.5         0        0         0
DSS_INDEX                      /u04/oracle/oradata/dss/dss_index01.dbf
       4,029       1    0.2     2.7         0        0         0
                               /u06/oracle/oradata/dss/dss_index02.dbf
       3,815       1    0.2     2.8         0        0         0
                               /u07/oracle/oradata/dss/dss_index03.dbf
       3,944       1    0.2     2.8         0        0         0
PERFSTAT                       /u05/oracle/oradata/dss/perfstat01.dbf
           3       0    0.0    10.0       803        0         0
SYSTEM                         /u01/oracle/oradata/dss/system01.dbf
          50       0    0.4     3.2       350        0         0
TEMP                           /u05/oracle/oradata/dss/temp1.dbf
      19,568       3    1.3    13.2    20,621        4         0
UNDOTBS1                       /u02/oracle/oradata/dss/undotbs101.dbf
           0       0                      60        0         0
                               /u04/oracle/oradata/dss/undotbs102.dbf
           0       0                      32        0         0
                               /u05/oracle/oradata/dss/undotbs103.dbf
           4       0    0.0     1.0       132        0         0
                 ------------------------------------------------------------
```

Looking at the STATSPACK from the SSD run 6 with reduced
buffer cache, there is not much of a shift in the profile based on

the loss of 500 megabytes of preloaded data. In fact, the hit ratio increases as is evidenced by the data in the following report.

```
Instance Efficiency Percentages (Target 100%)
~~~~~~~~~~~~~~~~~~~~~~~~~~~~~~~~~~~~~~~~~~~~~~~~
            Buffer Nowait %:  100.00     Redo NoWait %:  100.00
            Buffer  Hit   %:   20.31   In-memory Sort %:   99.66
            Library Hit   %:   93.73      Soft Parse %:    94.71
         Execute to Parse %:   58.87       Latch Hit %:   100.00
  Parse CPU to Parse Elapsd %:   4.53    % Non-Parse CPU:   99.98

  Shared Pool Statistics        Begin    End
                               ------   ------
                Memory Usage %:  33.65   37.94
       % SQL with executions>1:  52.23   60.09
       % Memory for SQL w/exec>1:  35.76   54.60

Top 5 Timed Events
~~~~~~~~~~~~~~~~~~                                          % Total
Event                                  Waits    Time (s) Ela Time
----------------------------------  -----------  --------  --------
CPU time                                           2,473     69.78
db file scattered read               1,313,555     1,026     28.95
db file parallel read                    6,564        26       .72
control file parallel write              1,194        10       .29
db file sequential read                 36,043         6       .17
                                    -----------------------------------
```

While the shift is there, it is only a couple of percentage points. As a reminder, here is the STATSPACK report for a run with the data files on the ATA drives.

```
Top 5 Timed Events
~~~~~~~~~~~~~~~~~~                                          % Total
Event                                  Waits    Time (s) Ela Time
----------------------------------  -----------  --------  --------
db file sequential read             93,211,687   398,236     96.80
CPU time                                          10,892      2.65
db file scattered read                 344,252     1,512       .37
control file parallel write            141,759       583       .14
latch free                               8,947        90       .02
                                    -----------------------------------
```

Compare the time in seconds waiting for the read events in the previous report with the ATA array results from the STATSPACK report shown above, and the total wait events and their associated wait times where reduced by a factor of 376 based on total wait time for I/O related events.

Consulting an end-user can help you assess
SSD performance improvements

Based on analysis of wait and file I/O characteristics, here are more examples of systems that may or may not benefit from a move to SSD.

When a System Won't Benefit From Moving to SSD

The move to SSD assets from standard SCSI, ATA or SATA disks can be of great benefit when it answers a specific performance problem related to disk I/O saturation. However, be careful when diagnosing the I/O related problems on a system.

🖫 STATSPACK reports

> The Code Depot has full listings of some example STATSPACK reports that will be reviewed here for clues on whether the system would benefit from utilizing SSD assets.

Look for high DB file waits!

Look at the events report below.

```
Top 5 Timed Events
~~~~~~~~~~~~~~~~~~~                                         % Total
Event                              Waits    Time (s) Ela Time
---------------------------------- ------------ ----------- --------
CPU time                                          1,127    73.25
global cache cr request            213,187         122     7.95
db file sequential read            152,521          96     6.27
control file sequential read       118,104          78     5.06
SQL*Net message from dblink            890          38     2.48
                                   ------------------------------------
```

The system referenced above spends 73 percent of its time in the CPU and only 11 percent of the time waiting on disks. Now if the system is tuned to eliminate the CPU bottle neck, then chances are the bottle neck will move to the disks. At that time the system would benefit from SSD technology. As the system referenced in the report above is configured now, moving to SSD could actually hurt performance as it would place more stress on the already over worked CPU assets. The system in the above report is a Real Application Cluster (RAC) system and the interconnects, which are shown by the global cache related waits, are a stress point. The interconnects would also be stressed by faster access to data.

In the next example report, the move to SSD might be beneficial since there is reserve CPU capacity of 40 percent and the system is spending the other wait time waiting on disks.

```
Top 5 Timed Events
~~~~~~~~~~~~~~~~~~~                                          % Total
Event                                    Waits   Time (s) Ela Time
------------------------------------- ------------ ----------- --------
CPU time                                           1,300    60.46
db file sequential read                342,625       616    28.67
db file scattered read                  12,986        66     3.07
log file parallel write                  2,889        65     3.03
db file parallel write                   1,080        59     2.75
                                      -------------------------------------
```

The system reference above is showing index and table stress as well as stress on log files. Assuming that the sample amount of time in the STATSPACK is representative of the overall system performance, it is necessary to look further to see whether tables or indexes should be moved to the SSD asset. Here is the file I/O profile from this same report.

```
Tablespace
------------------------------
               Av     Av    Av                    Av       Buffer Av Buf
       Reads Reads/s Rd(ms) Blks/Rd   Writes Writes/s  Waits Wt(ms)
------------- ------- ------ ------- ------------ -------- ---------- ------
SRCD
       12,680      4    6.7    1.0    18,943       6         0    0.0
SYSTEM
       30,282     10    3.0    2.5       623       0         0    0.0
UNDOTBS1
           14      0   35.7    1.0    28,733       9         0    0.0
SRCX
        2,799      1    4.5    1.0    18,038       6         0    0.0
NOMADD
       16,604      5    1.8    1.0         8       0         0    0.0
TST_GLOBALX
        7,560      2    1.6    1.0        18       0         0    0.0
TST_GLOBALD
        6,242      2    2.0    1.2        36       0         0    0.0
XDB
        5,636      2    1.5    1.0         4       0         0    0.0
REEX
        4,240      1    2.0    1.0         4       0         0    0.0
ZENX
        3,812      1    2.1    1.0         4       0         0    0.0
ESRX
        3,656      1    1.6    1.0         4       0         0    0.0
```

The heavy-hitters are the SRCD, SYSTEM, NOMAD, TST_GLOBALX and TST_GLOBALD tablespaces. The actual report from which this listing is extracted is over 10 pages long for this section on datafiles, but these are the largest contributors to the I/O profile. Analysis of the system showed improper use of the SYSTEM tablespace. Once this was corrected, moving the remaining heavy hitters to an SSD asset would do the following for this system:

- Shift the load to the CPUs

- Reduce I/O stress on the I/O subsystem allowing other datafiles to be accessed more efficiently.

- Speed access to the data/indexes contained in the moved datafiles.

Notice that one of the other waits deals with redo log files, specifically log file parallel write. Since this is a log file write specific wait, moving the redo logs would also show some benefit, but not as great as that shown by moving tables and indexes. The following report shows a false-positive indicator for use of SSD.

```
Top 5 Timed Events
~~~~~~~~~~~~~~~~~~~                                            % Total
Event                                     Waits   Time (s) Ela Time
------------------------------------- ----------- ----------- --------
db file sequential read                 6,261,550         691    96.72
control file parallel write                 1,274          19     2.73
CPU time                                                     2      .24
db file parallel write                          28           1      .14
db file scattered read                       2,248           1      .12
                                      ------------ ----------- --------
```

False-positive in this case is indicated because looking at the STATSPACK seems to suggest that the database is doing a lot of full table scans and that this is 96-97 percent of the wait times. Typically this would indicate that a move to SSD would be beneficial. However, look at the entire report as a whole. The header for the file is shown next.

```
STATSPACK report for

DB Name        DB Id      Instance      Inst Num Release      Cluster Host
------------   -----------  ------------  -------- -----------  ------- -----------
-
TSTPRD         3265066449 tstprd              1 9.2.0.3.0    NO      test08

               Snap Id    Snap Time      Sessions Curs/Sess Comment
               -------  -----------------  -------- --------- -------------------
Begin Snap:         3 09-Nov-03 13:20:20      10      2.1
  End Snap:         4 09-Nov-03 14:26:01      10      2.1
  Elapsed:                  65.68 (mins)

Cache Sizes (end)
~~~~~~~~~~~~~~~~~
            Buffer Cache:        24M   Std Block Size:         8K
         Shared Pool Size:       48M      Log Buffer:        512K
```

Notice the tiny size of the buffer cache and shared pool, and also the restricted time period monitored. Unless the server has severe memory limitations, the company using this database would be better off increasing the memory allocated to the instance and then looking at SSD if the waits are still an issue. The small elapsed time indicates that this STATSPACK run was probably for a specific transaction and is not indicative of full system load.

Conclusion

To be beneficial, STATSPACK reports must not target a specific transaction but should look at overall system load. Also be aware of the memory allocation profile for the database on which the STATSPACK was run. If the memory is a choke point and there are sufficient resources available, tune there first, then evaluate for SSD suitability.

SSD assets will only help if a system is experiencing I/O contention. And then it will only give back the performance lost from those I/O activities by replacing memory I/Os for physical I/Os. As in the benchmark study where system load is predominately I/O related, significant performance gains can be realized.

Following this chapter are the Appendices which include script listings and expanded data and statistic listings.

Example Scripts

Appendix A

Appendix A lists the scripts used to create indexes and the two sets of queries. The first used for SSD testing and the second, used for ATA testing.

Always use lots of example tests in any benchmark!

Index Creation Script

```
--  ***************************************************
-- Copyright © 2003 by Rampant TechPress
-- This script is free for non-commercial purposes
-- with no warranties.  Use at your own risk.
--
-- To license this script for a commercial purpose,
-- contact info@rampant.cc
--  ***************************************************

set echo on
spool index_create.log
select to_char(sysdate,'dd-mon-yyyy hh24:mi.ss') from dual;
create index lineitem_sd on lineitem(l_shipdate)
tablespace dss_index nologging;
select to_char(sysdate,'dd-mon-yyyy hh24:mi.ss') from dual;
create index part_sz on part(p_size)
tablespace dss_index nologging;
select to_char(sysdate,'dd-mon-yyyy hh24:mi.ss') from dual;
create index part_typ on part(p_type)
tablespace dss_index nologging;
select to_char(sysdate,'dd-mon-yyyy hh24:mi.ss') from dual;
create index cust_mktseg on customer(c_mktsegment)
tablespace dss_index nologging;
select to_char(sysdate,'dd-mon-yyyy hh24:mi.ss') from dual;
create index orders_odat on orders(o_orderdate)
tablespace dss_index nologging;
select to_char(sysdate,'dd-mon-yyyy hh24:mi.ss') from dual;
create index lineitem_supk on lineitem(l_suppkey)
tablespace dss_index nologging;
select to_char(sysdate,'dd-mon-yyyy hh24:mi.ss') from dual;
create index lineitem_ok on lineitem(l_orderkey)
tablespace dss_index nologging;
select to_char(sysdate,'dd-mon-yyyy hh24:mi.ss') from dual;
create index supp_nk on supplier(s_nationkey)
tablespace dss_index nologging;
select to_char(sysdate,'dd-mon-yyyy hh24:mi.ss') from dual;
create index cust_nk on customer(c_nationkey)
tablespace dss_index nologging;
select to_char(sysdate,'dd-mon-yyyy hh24:mi.ss') from dual;
create index lineitem_sm on lineitem(l_shipmode)
tablespace dss_index nologging;
select to_char(sysdate,'dd-mon-yyyy hh24:mi.ss') from dual;
create index part_brd on part(p_brand)
tablespace dss_index nologging;
select to_char(sysdate,'dd-mon-yyyy hh24:mi.ss') from dual;
create index part_typ on part(p_type)
tablespace dss_index nologging;
select to_char(sysdate,'dd-mon-yyyy hh24:mi.ss') from dual;
```

```
create index part_con on part(p_container)
tablespace dss_index nologging;
select to_char(sysdate,'dd-mon-yyyy hh24:mi.ss') from dual;
create index lineitem_si on lineitem(l_shipinstruct)
tablespace dss_index nologging;
select to_char(sysdate,'dd-mon-yyyy hh24:mi.ss') from dual;
create index partsupp_sk on partsupp(ps_suppkey)
tablespace dss_index nologging;
select to_char(sysdate,'dd-mon-yyyy hh24:mi.ss') from dual;
create index lineitem_prtk on lineitem(l_partkey)
tablespace dss_index nologging;
select to_char(sysdate,'dd-mon-yyyy hh24:mi.ss') from dual;
spool off;
```

SSD Queries Script

First the query script used for the SSD queries. Notice that the addition of extra login statements is not needed:

💾 SSD Queries Script

```
-- **************************************************
-- Copyright © 2003 by Rampant TechPress
-- This script is free for non-commercial purposes
-- with no warranties.  Use at your own risk.
--
-- To license this script for a commercial purpose,
-- contact info@rampant.cc
-- **************************************************

-- using 1119557751 as a seed to the RNG
set lines 1000
set pages 58
set timing on
ttitle 'Query 1 output'
spool query1.lst
select to_char(sysdate,'dd-mon-yyyy hh24:mi') from dual;
select
    l_returnflag,
    l_linestatus,
    sum(l_quantity) as sum_qty,
    sum(l_extendedprice) as sum_base_price,
    sum(l_extendedprice * (1 - l_discount)) as sum_disc_price,
    sum(l_extendedprice * (1 - l_discount) * (1 + l_tax)) as
sum_charge,
    avg(l_quantity) as avg_qty,
    avg(l_extendedprice) as avg_price,
    avg(l_discount) as avg_disc,
    count(*) as count_order
from
    lineitem
where
    l_shipdate <= date '1998-12-01' - interval '76' day (3)
group by
    l_returnflag,
    l_linestatus
order by
    l_returnflag,
    l_linestatus;
spool off

ttitle 'Query 2 output'
spool query2.lst

select
```

```
        s_acctbal,
        s_name,
        n_name,
        p_partkey,
        p_mfgr,
        s_address,
        s_phone,
        s_comment
from
        part,
        supplier,
        partsupp,
        nation,
        region
where
        p_partkey = ps_partkey
        and s_suppkey = ps_suppkey
        and p_size = 9
        and p_type like '%STEEL'
        and s_nationkey = n_nationkey
        and n_regionkey = r_regionkey
        and r_name = 'AFRICA'
        and ps_supplycost = (
                select
                        min(ps_supplycost)
                from
                        partsupp,
                        supplier,
                        nation,
                        region
                where
                        p_partkey = ps_partkey
                        and s_suppkey = ps_suppkey
                        and s_nationkey = n_nationkey
                        and n_regionkey = r_regionkey
                        and r_name = 'AFRICA'
        )
and rownum<101
order by
        s_acctbal desc,
        n_name,
        s_name,
        p_partkey;
spool off;

ttitle 'Query 3 output'
spool query3.lst

select
        l_orderkey,
        sum(l_extendedprice * (1 - l_discount)) as revenue,
        o_orderdate,
        o_shippriority
from
        customer,
        orders,
        lineitem
```

```
where
    c_mktsegment = 'AUTOMOBILE'
    and c_custkey = o_custkey
    and l_orderkey = o_orderkey
    and o_orderdate < date '1995-03-04'
    and l_shipdate > date '1995-03-04'
        and rownum<11
group by
    l_orderkey,
    o_orderdate,
    o_shippriority
order by
    revenue desc,
    o_orderdate;
spool off

ttitle 'Query 4 output'
spool query4.lst

select
    o_orderpriority,
    count(*) as order_count
from
    orders
where
    o_orderdate >= date '1993-09-01'
    and o_orderdate < date '1993-09-01' + interval '3' month
    and exists (
            select
                    *
            from
                    lineitem
            where
                    l_orderkey = o_orderkey
                    and l_commitdate < l_receiptdate
    )
group by
    o_orderpriority
order by
    o_orderpriority;
spool off

ttitle 'Query 5 output'
spool query5.lst

select
    n_name,
    sum(l_extendedprice * (1 - l_discount)) as revenue
from
    customer,
    orders,
    lineitem,
    supplier,
    nation,
    region
where
    c_custkey = o_custkey
```

```
        and l_orderkey = o_orderkey
        and l_suppkey = s_suppkey
        and c_nationkey = s_nationkey
        and s_nationkey = n_nationkey
        and n_regionkey = r_regionkey
        and r_name = 'AMERICA'
        and o_orderdate >= date '1996-01-01'
        and o_orderdate < date '1996-01-01' + interval '1' year
group by
    n_name
order by
    revenue desc;

spool off

ttitle 'Query 6 output'
spool query6.lst

select
    sum(l_extendedprice * l_discount) as revenue
from
    lineitem
where
    l_shipdate >= date '1996-01-01'
    and l_shipdate < date '1996-01-01' + interval '1' year
    and l_discount between 0.07 - 0.01 and 0.07 + 0.01
    and l_quantity < 24;

spool off

ttitle 'Query 7 output'
spool query7.lst


select
    supp_nation,
    cust_nation,
    l_year,
    sum(volume)  revenue
from
    (
            select
                    n1.n_name   supp_nation,
                    n2.n_name   cust_nation,
                    extract(year from l_shipdate)  l_year,
                    l_extendedprice * (1 - l_discount)  volume
            from
                    supplier,
                    lineitem,
                    orders,
                    customer,
                    nation n1,
                    nation n2
            where
                    s_suppkey = l_suppkey
                    and o_orderkey = l_orderkey
                    and c_custkey = o_custkey
```

```
                    and s_nationkey = n1.n_nationkey
                    and c_nationkey = n2.n_nationkey
                    and (
                            (n1.n_name = 'MOZAMBIQUE' and n2.n_name =
'INDONESIA')
                            or (n1.n_name = 'INDONESIA' and n2.n_name
= 'MOZAMBIQUE')
                    )
                    and l_shipdate between to_date( '1995-01-
01','yyyy-mm-dd') and to_date( '1996-12-31','yyyy-mm-dd')
    ) shipping
group by
    supp_nation,
    cust_nation,
    l_year
order by
    supp_nation,
    cust_nation,
    l_year;

spool off

ttitle 'Query 7 output'
spool query7.lst


select
    o_year,
    sum(case
            when nation = 'INDONESIA' then volume
            else 0
    end) / sum(volume) mkt_share
from
    (
        select
                extract(year from o_orderdate) o_year,
                l_extendedprice * (1 - l_discount) volume,
                n2.n_name nation
        from
                part,
                supplier,
                lineitem,
                orders,
                customer,
                nation n1,
                nation n2,
                region
        where
                p_partkey = l_partkey
                and s_suppkey = l_suppkey
                and l_orderkey = o_orderkey
                and o_custkey = c_custkey
                and c_nationkey = n1.n_nationkey
                and n1.n_regionkey = r_regionkey
                and r_name = 'ASIA'
                and s_nationkey = n2.n_nationkey
```

```
                    and o_orderdate between  to_date( '1995-01-
01','yyyy-mm-dd') and to_date( '1996-12-31','yyyy-mm-dd')
                    and p_type = 'MEDIUM POLISHED STEEL'
    ) all_nations
group by
    o_year
order by
    o_year;

spool off

ttitle 'Query 8 output'
spool query8.lst


select
    nation,
    o_year,
    sum(amount) sum_profit
from
    (
        select
            n_name nation,
            extract(year from o_orderdate) o_year,
            l_extendedprice * (1 - l_discount) -
ps_supplycost * l_quantity as amount
        from
            part,
            supplier,
            lineitem,
            partsupp,
            orders,
            nation
        where
            s_suppkey = l_suppkey
            and ps_suppkey = l_suppkey
            and ps_partkey = l_partkey
            and p_partkey = l_partkey
            and o_orderkey = l_orderkey
            and s_nationkey = n_nationkey
            and p_name like '%lavender%'
    ) profit
group by
    nation,
    o_year
order by
    nation,
    o_year desc;

spool off

ttitle 'Query 9 output'
spool query9.lst


select
    c_custkey,
```

```
    c_name,
    sum(l_extendedprice * (1 - l_discount)) revenue,
    c_acctbal,
    n_name,
    c_address,
    c_phone,
    c_comment
from
    customer,
    orders,
    lineitem,
    nation
where
    c_custkey = o_custkey
    and l_orderkey = o_orderkey
    and o_orderdate >= date '1993-11-01'
    and o_orderdate < date '1993-11-01' + interval '3' month
    and l_returnflag = 'R'
    and c_nationkey = n_nationkey
        and rownum<21
group by
    c_custkey,
    c_name,
    c_acctbal,
    c_phone,
    n_name,
    c_address,
    c_comment
order by
    revenue desc;

spool off

ttitle 'Query 10 output'
spool query10.lst


select
    ps_partkey,
    sum(ps_supplycost * ps_availqty) value
from
    partsupp,
    supplier,
    nation
where
    ps_suppkey = s_suppkey
    and s_nationkey = n_nationkey
    and n_name = 'INDIA'
group by
    ps_partkey having
            sum(ps_supplycost * ps_availqty) > (
                    select
                            sum(ps_supplycost * ps_availqty) *
0.0001000000
                    from
                            partsupp,
                            supplier,
```

```
                         nation
              where
                         ps_suppkey = s_suppkey
                         and s_nationkey = n_nationkey
                         and n_name = 'INDIA'
         )
order by
    value desc;

spool off

ttitle 'Query 11 output'
spool query11.lst


select
    l_shipmode,
    sum(case
           when o_orderpriority = '1-URGENT'
                or o_orderpriority = '2-HIGH'
                then 1
           else 0
    end) as high_line_count,
    sum(case
           when o_orderpriority <> '1-URGENT'
                and o_orderpriority <> '2-HIGH'
                then 1
           else 0
    end) as low_line_count
from
    orders,
    lineitem
where
    o_orderkey = l_orderkey
    and l_shipmode in ('REG AIR', 'RAIL')
    and l_commitdate < l_receiptdate
    and l_shipdate < l_commitdate
    and l_receiptdate >= to_date( '1997-01-01','yyyy-mm-dd')
    and l_receiptdate < date '1997-01-01' + interval '1' year
group by
    l_shipmode
order by
    l_shipmode;

spool off

ttitle 'Query 12 output'
spool query12.lst


select
    c_count,
    count(*)  custdist
from
    (
         select
              c_custkey,
```

```
                        count(o_orderkey) c_count
              from
                     customer left outer join orders on
                           c_custkey = o_custkey
                           and o_comment not like
'%pending%deposits%'
              group by
                     c_custkey
     ) c_orders
group by
     c_count
order by
     custdist desc,
     c_count desc;

spool off

ttitle 'Query 13 output'
spool query13.lst


select
     100.00 * sum(case
              when p_type like 'PROMO%'
                     then l_extendedprice * (1 - l_discount)
              else 0
     end) / sum(l_extendedprice * (1 - l_discount)) as promo_revenue
from
     lineitem,
     part
where
     l_partkey = p_partkey
     and l_shipdate >= to_date( '1997-07-01','yyyy-mm-dd')
     and l_shipdate < date '1997-07-01' + interval '1' month;


create view revenue0 (supplier_no, total_revenue) as
     select
              l_suppkey,
              sum(l_extendedprice * (1 - l_discount))
     from
              lineitem
     where
              l_shipdate >= to_date( '1993-10-01','yyyy-mm-dd')
              and l_shipdate < date '1993-10-01' + interval '3' month
     group by
              l_suppkey;


select
     s_suppkey,
     s_name,
     s_address,
     s_phone,
     total_revenue
from
     supplier,
```

```
        revenue0
where
    s_suppkey = supplier_no
    and total_revenue = (
            select
                    max(total_revenue)
            from
                    revenue0
    )
order by
    s_suppkey;

drop view revenue0;

spool off

ttitle 'Query 14 output'
spool query4.lst


select
    p_brand,
    p_type,
    p_size,
    count(distinct ps_suppkey) as supplier_cnt
from
    partsupp,
    part
where
    p_partkey = ps_partkey
    and p_brand <> 'Brand#11'
    and p_type not like 'LARGE BRUSHED%'
    and p_size in (8, 24, 15, 30, 25, 45, 13, 38)
    and ps_suppkey not in (
            select
                    s_suppkey
            from
                    supplier
            where
                    s_comment like '%Customer%Complaints%'
    )
group by
    p_brand,
    p_type,
    p_size
order by
    supplier_cnt desc,
    p_brand,
    p_type,
    p_size;

spool off

ttitle 'Query 14 output'
spool query14.lst
```

```
select
    sum(l_extendedprice) / 7.0 as avg_yearly
from
    lineitem,
    part
where
    p_partkey = l_partkey
    and p_brand = 'Brand#14'
    and p_container = 'SM PACK'
    and l_quantity < (
            select
                    0.2 * avg(l_quantity)
            from
                    lineitem
            where
                    l_partkey = p_partkey
    );

spool off

ttitle 'Query 15 output'
spool query15.lst


select
    c_name,
    c_custkey,
    o_orderkey,
    o_orderdate,
    o_totalprice,
    sum(l_quantity)
from
    customer,
    orders,
    lineitem
where
    o_orderkey in (
            select
                    l_orderkey
            from
                    lineitem
            group by
                    l_orderkey having
                            sum(l_quantity) > 314
    )
    and c_custkey = o_custkey
    and o_orderkey = l_orderkey
        and rownum<101
group by
    c_name,
    c_custkey,
    o_orderkey,
    o_orderdate,
    o_totalprice
order by
    o_totalprice desc,
    o_orderdate;
```

Appendix A

143

```
spool off

ttitle 'Query 16 output'
spool query16.lst


select
    sum(l_extendedprice* (1 - l_discount)) revenue
from
    lineitem,
    part
where
    (
            p_partkey = l_partkey
            and p_brand = 'Brand#14'
            and p_container in ('SM CASE', 'SM BOX', 'SM PACK', 'SM
PKG')
            and l_quantity >= 2 and l_quantity <= 2 + 10
            and p_size between 1 and 5
            and l_shipmode in ('AIR', 'AIR REG')
            and l_shipinstruct = 'DELIVER IN PERSON'
    )
    or
    (
            p_partkey = l_partkey
            and p_brand = 'Brand#24'
            and p_container in ('MED BAG', 'MED BOX', 'MED PKG',
'MED PACK')
            and l_quantity >= 12 and l_quantity <= 12 + 10
            and p_size between 1 and 10
            and l_shipmode in ('AIR', 'AIR REG')
            and l_shipinstruct = 'DELIVER IN PERSON'
    )
    or
    (
            p_partkey = l_partkey
            and p_brand = 'Brand#35'
            and p_container in ('LG CASE', 'LG BOX', 'LG PACK', 'LG
PKG')
            and l_quantity >= 28 and l_quantity <= 28 + 10
            and p_size between 1 and 15
            and l_shipmode in ('AIR', 'AIR REG')
            and l_shipinstruct = 'DELIVER IN PERSON'
    );

spool off

ttitle 'Query 17 output'
spool query17.lst


select
    s_name,
    s_address
from
    supplier,
```

```
        nation
where
    s_suppkey in (
            select
                    ps_suppkey
            from
                    partsupp
            where
                    ps_partkey in (
                            select
                                    p_partkey
                            from
                                    part
                            where
                                    p_name like 'orange%'
                    )
                    and ps_availqty > (
                            select
                                    0.5 * sum(l_quantity)
                            from
                                    lineitem
                            where
                                    l_partkey = ps_partkey
                                    and l_suppkey = ps_suppkey
                                    and l_shipdate >= to_date( '1994-
01-01','yyyy-mm-dd')
                                    and l_shipdate < date '1994-01-01'
+ interval '1' year
                    )
    )
    and s_nationkey = n_nationkey
    and n_name = 'MOZAMBIQUE'
order by
    s_name;

spool off

ttitle 'Query 18 output'
spool query18.lst


select
    s_name,
    count(*) numwait
from
    supplier,
    lineitem l1,
    orders,
    nation
where
    s_suppkey = l1.l_suppkey
    and o_orderkey = l1.l_orderkey
    and o_orderstatus = 'F'
    and l1.l_receiptdate > l1.l_commitdate
    and exists (
            select
                    *
```

```
                from
                        lineitem l2
                where
                        l2.1_orderkey = l1.1_orderkey
                        and l2.1_suppkey <> l1.1_suppkey
        )
        and not exists (
                select
                        *
                from
                        lineitem l3
                where
                        l3.1_orderkey = l1.1_orderkey
                        and l3.1_suppkey <> l1.1_suppkey
                        and l3.1_receiptdate > l3.1_commitdate
        )
        and s_nationkey = n_nationkey
        and n_name = 'GERMANY'
            and rownum<101
group by
        s_name
order by
        numwait desc,
        s_name;

spool off

ttitle 'Query 19 output'
spool query19.1st


select
        cntrycode,
        count(*) numcust,
        sum(c_acctbal) totacctbal
from
        (
                select
                        substr(c_phone, 1, 2) cntrycode,
                        c_acctbal
                from
                        customer
                where
                        substr(c_phone,1,2) in
                                ('30', '22', '32', '13', '28', '21',
'24')
                        and c_acctbal > (
                                select
                                        avg(c_acctbal)
                                from
                                        customer
                                where
                                        c_acctbal > 0.00
                                        and substr(c_phone,1,2) in
                                                ('30', '22', '32', '13',
'28', '21', '24')
                        )
```

```
                    and not exists (
                        select
                                    *
                        from
                                    orders
                        where
                                    o_custkey = c_custkey
                    )
        ) custsale
group by
    cntrycode
order by
    cntrycode;
select to_char(sysdate,'dd-mon-yyyy hh24:mi') from dual;

spool off
ttitle off
set timing off
```

SCSI/ATA Queries Script

Now the modified script for the SCSI and ATA runs. The script was modified to do a re-connect between queries to prevent undo and temporary segment issues.

💾 **Queries Script**

```
--  ***************************************************
-- Copyright © 2003 by Rampant TechPress
-- This script is free for non-commercial purposes
-- with no warranties.  Use at your own risk.
--
-- To license this script for a commercial purpose,
-- contact info@rampant.cc
--  ***************************************************

-- using 1119557751 as a seed to the RNG
set lines 1000
set pages 58
set timing on
-- Note: Had to comment out query1 as it exceeded 24 hour runtime
limit
--ttitle 'Query 1 output'
--spool query1.lst
--select to_char(sysdate,'dd-mon-yyyy hh24:mi') from dual;
--select
--   l_returnflag,
--   l_linestatus,
--   sum(l_quantity) as sum_qty,
--   sum(l_extendedprice) as sum_base_price,
--   sum(l_extendedprice * (1 - l_discount)) as sum_disc_price,
--   sum(l_extendedprice * (1 - l_discount) * (1 + l_tax)) as
sum_charge,
--   avg(l_quantity) as avg_qty,
--   avg(l_extendedprice) as avg_price,
--   avg(l_discount) as avg_disc,
--   count(*) as count_order
--from
--   lineitem
--where
--   l_shipdate <= date '1998-12-01' - interval '76' day (3)
--group by
--   l_returnflag,
--   l_linestatus
--order by
--   l_returnflag,
--   l_linestatus;
--spool off
connect dss_admin/dss_admin
```

```
set lines 1000
set pages 58
set timing on
ttitle 'Query 2 output'
spool query2.lst

select
    s_acctbal,
    s_name,
    n_name,
    p_partkey,
    p_mfgr,
    s_address,
    s_phone,
    s_comment
from
    part,
    supplier,
    partsupp,
    nation,
    region
where
    p_partkey = ps_partkey
    and s_suppkey = ps_suppkey
    and p_size = 9
    and p_type like '%STEEL'
    and s_nationkey = n_nationkey
    and n_regionkey = r_regionkey
    and r_name = 'AFRICA'
    and ps_supplycost = (
            select
                    min(ps_supplycost)
            from
                    partsupp,
                    supplier,
                    nation,
                    region
            where
                    p_partkey = ps_partkey
                    and s_suppkey = ps_suppkey
                    and s_nationkey = n_nationkey
                    and n_regionkey = r_regionkey
                    and r_name = 'AFRICA'
    )
and rownum<101
order by
    s_acctbal desc,
    n_name,
    s_name,
    p_partkey;
spool off;
connect dss_admin/dss_admin
set lines 1000
set pages 58
set timing on
ttitle 'Query 3 output'
spool query3.lst
```

```
select
    l_orderkey,
    sum(l_extendedprice * (1 - l_discount)) as revenue,
    o_orderdate,
    o_shippriority
from
    customer,
    orders,
    lineitem
where
    c_mktsegment = 'AUTOMOBILE'
    and c_custkey = o_custkey
    and l_orderkey = o_orderkey
    and o_orderdate < date '1995-03-04'
    and l_shipdate > date '1995-03-04'
        and rownum<11
group by
    l_orderkey,
    o_orderdate,
    o_shippriority
order by
    revenue desc,
    o_orderdate;
spool off

connect dss_admin/dss_admin
set lines 1000
set pages 58
set timing on
ttitle 'Query 4 output'
spool query4.lst

select
    o_orderpriority,
    count(*) as order_count
from
    orders
where
    o_orderdate >= date '1993-09-01'
    and o_orderdate < date '1993-09-01' + interval '3' month
    and exists (
            select
                    *
            from
                    lineitem
            where
                    l_orderkey = o_orderkey
                    and l_commitdate < l_receiptdate
    )
group by
    o_orderpriority
order by
    o_orderpriority;
spool off

connect dss_admin/dss_admin
```

```
set lines 1000
set pages 58
set timing on
ttitle 'Query 5 output'
spool query5.lst

select
    n_name,
    sum(l_extendedprice * (1 - l_discount)) as revenue
from
    customer,
    orders,
    lineitem,
    supplier,
    nation,
    region
where
    c_custkey = o_custkey
    and l_orderkey = o_orderkey
    and l_suppkey = s_suppkey
    and c_nationkey = s_nationkey
    and s_nationkey = n_nationkey
    and n_regionkey = r_regionkey
    and r_name = 'AMERICA'
    and o_orderdate >= date '1996-01-01'
    and o_orderdate < date '1996-01-01' + interval '1' year
group by
    n_name
order by
    revenue desc;

spool off

connect dss_admin/dss_admin
set lines 1000
set pages 58
set timing on
ttitle 'Query 6 output'
spool query6.lst

select
    sum(l_extendedprice * l_discount) as revenue
from
    lineitem
where
    l_shipdate >= date '1996-01-01'
    and l_shipdate < date '1996-01-01' + interval '1' year
    and l_discount between 0.07 - 0.01 and 0.07 + 0.01
    and l_quantity < 24;

spool off

connect dss_admin/dss_admin
set lines 1000
set pages 58
set timing on
ttitle 'Query 7 output'
```

```
spool query7.1st


select
    supp_nation,
    cust_nation,
    l_year,
    sum(volume)  revenue
from
    (
            select
                    n1.n_name  supp_nation,
                    n2.n_name  cust_nation,
                    extract(year from l_shipdate)  l_year,
                    l_extendedprice * (1 - l_discount)  volume
            from
                    supplier,
                    lineitem,
                    orders,
                    customer,
                    nation n1,
                    nation n2
            where
                    s_suppkey = l_suppkey
                    and o_orderkey = l_orderkey
                    and c_custkey = o_custkey
                    and s_nationkey = n1.n_nationkey
                    and c_nationkey = n2.n_nationkey
                    and (
                            (n1.n_name = 'MOZAMBIQUE' and n2.n_name =
'INDONESIA')
                            or (n1.n_name = 'INDONESIA' and n2.n_name
= 'MOZAMBIQUE')
                    )
                    and l_shipdate between to_date( '1995-01-
01','yyyy-mm-dd') and to_date( '1996-12-31','yyyy-mm-dd')
    )  shipping
group by
    supp_nation,
    cust_nation,
    l_year
order by
    supp_nation,
    cust_nation,
    l_year;

spool off

connect dss_admin/dss_admin
set lines 1000
set pages 58
set timing on
ttitle 'Query 7a output'
spool query7a.1st


select
```

```
     o_year,
     sum(case
             when nation = 'INDONESIA' then volume
             else 0
     end) / sum(volume) mkt_share
from
     (
             select
                     extract(year from o_orderdate) o_year,
                     l_extendedprice * (1 - l_discount) volume,
                     n2.n_name nation
             from
                     part,
                     supplier,
                     lineitem,
                     orders,
                     customer,
                     nation n1,
                     nation n2,
                     region
             where
                     p_partkey = l_partkey
                     and s_suppkey = l_suppkey
                     and l_orderkey = o_orderkey
                     and o_custkey = c_custkey
                     and c_nationkey = n1.n_nationkey
                     and n1.n_regionkey = r_regionkey
                     and r_name = 'ASIA'
                     and s_nationkey = n2.n_nationkey
                     and o_orderdate between  to_date( '1995-01-
01','yyyy-mm-dd') and to_date( '1996-12-31','yyyy-mm-dd')
                     and p_type = 'MEDIUM POLISHED STEEL'
     ) all_nations
group by
     o_year
order by
     o_year;

spool off

connect dss_admin/dss_admin
set lines 1000
set pages 58
set timing on
ttitle 'Query 8 output'
spool query8.lst


select
     nation,
     o_year,
     sum(amount) sum_profit
from
     (
             select
                     n_name nation,
                     extract(year from o_orderdate) o_year,
```

```
                       l_extendedprice * (1 - l_discount) -
ps_supplycost * l_quantity as amount
             from
                     part,
                     supplier,
                     lineitem,
                     partsupp,
                     orders,
                     nation
           where
                     s_suppkey = l_suppkey
                     and ps_suppkey = l_suppkey
                     and ps_partkey = l_partkey
                     and p_partkey = l_partkey
                     and o_orderkey = l_orderkey
                     and s_nationkey = n_nationkey
                     and p_name like '%lavender%'
       ) profit
group by
     nation,
     o_year
order by
     nation,
     o_year desc;

spool off

connect dss_admin/dss_admin
set lines 1000
set pages 58
set timing on
ttitle 'Query 9 output'
spool query9.lst


select
     c_custkey,
     c_name,
     sum(l_extendedprice * (1 - l_discount)) revenue,
     c_acctbal,
     n_name,
     c_address,
     c_phone,
     c_comment
from
     customer,
     orders,
     lineitem,
     nation
where
     c_custkey = o_custkey
     and l_orderkey = o_orderkey
     and o_orderdate >= date '1993-11-01'
     and o_orderdate < date '1993-11-01' + interval '3' month
     and l_returnflag = 'R'
     and c_nationkey = n_nationkey
        and rownum<21
```

```
group by
    c_custkey,
    c_name,
    c_acctbal,
    c_phone,
    n_name,
    c_address,
    c_comment
order by
    revenue desc;
spool off

connect dss_admin/dss_admin
set lines 1000
set pages 58
set timing on
ttitle 'Query 10 output'
spool query10.lst

select
    ps_partkey,
    sum(ps_supplycost * ps_availqty) value
from
    partsupp,
    supplier,
    nation
where
    ps_suppkey = s_suppkey
    and s_nationkey = n_nationkey
    and n_name = 'INDIA'
group by
    ps_partkey having
        sum(ps_supplycost * ps_availqty) > (
            select
                sum(ps_supplycost * ps_availqty) *
0.0001000000
            from
                partsupp,
                supplier,
                nation
            where
                ps_suppkey = s_suppkey
                and s_nationkey = n_nationkey
                and n_name = 'INDIA'
        )
order by
    value desc;

spool off

connect dss_admin/dss_admin
set lines 1000
set pages 58
set timing on
ttitle 'Query 11 output'
spool query11.lst
```

```
select
    l_shipmode,
    sum(case
            when o_orderpriority = '1-URGENT'
                    or o_orderpriority = '2-HIGH'
                    then 1
            else 0
    end) as high_line_count,
    sum(case
            when o_orderpriority <> '1-URGENT'
                    and o_orderpriority <> '2-HIGH'
                    then 1
            else 0
    end) as low_line_count
from
    orders,
    lineitem
where
    o_orderkey = l_orderkey
    and l_shipmode in ('REG AIR', 'RAIL')
    and l_commitdate < l_receiptdate
    and l_shipdate < l_commitdate
    and l_receiptdate >= to_date( '1997-01-01','yyyy-mm-dd')
    and l_receiptdate < date '1997-01-01' + interval '1' year
group by
    l_shipmode
order by
    l_shipmode;

spool off

connect dss_admin/dss_admin
set lines 1000
set pages 58
set timing on
ttitle 'Query 12 output'
spool query12.lst


select
    c_count,
    count(*)  custdist
from
    (
            select
                    c_custkey,
                    count(o_orderkey) c_count
            from
                    customer left outer join orders on
                            c_custkey = o_custkey
                            and o_comment not like
'%pending%deposits%'
            group by
                    c_custkey
    ) c_orders
group by
```

Oracle Solid State Disk Tuning

```
        c_count
order by
    custdist desc,
    c_count desc;

spool off

connect dss_admin/dss_admin
set lines 1000
set pages 58
set timing on
ttitle 'Query 13 output'
spool query13.lst


select
    100.00 * sum(case
            when p_type like 'PROMO%'
                    then l_extendedprice * (1 - l_discount)
            else 0
    end) / sum(l_extendedprice * (1 - l_discount)) as promo_revenue
from
    lineitem,
    part
where
    l_partkey = p_partkey
    and l_shipdate >= to_date( '1997-07-01','yyyy-mm-dd')
    and l_shipdate < date '1997-07-01' + interval '1' month;


create view revenue0 (supplier_no, total_revenue) as
    select
            l_suppkey,
            sum(l_extendedprice * (1 - l_discount))
    from
            lineitem
    where
            l_shipdate >= to_date( '1993-10-01','yyyy-mm-dd')
            and l_shipdate < date '1993-10-01' + interval '3' month
    group by
            l_suppkey;

connect dss_admin/dss_admin
set lines 1000
set pages 58
set timing on
ttitle 'Query 13a Output'
spool query13a.lst
select
    s_suppkey,
    s_name,
    s_address,
    s_phone,
    total_revenue
from
    supplier,
    revenue0
```

```
where
    s_suppkey = supplier_no
    and total_revenue = (
            select
                    max(total_revenue)
            from
                    revenue0
    )
order by
    s_suppkey;

drop view revenue0;

spool off

connect dss_admin/dss_admin
set lines 1000
set pages 58
set timing on
ttitle 'Query 14 output'
spool query4.1st


select
    p_brand,
    p_type,
    p_size,
    count(distinct ps_suppkey) as supplier_cnt
from
    partsupp,
    part
where
    p_partkey = ps_partkey
    and p_brand <> 'Brand#11'
    and p_type not like 'LARGE BRUSHED%'
    and p_size in (8, 24, 15, 30, 25, 45, 13, 38)
    and ps_suppkey not in (
            select
                    s_suppkey
            from
                    supplier
            where
                    s_comment like '%Customer%Complaints%'
    )
group by
    p_brand,
    p_type,
    p_size
order by
    supplier_cnt desc,
    p_brand,
    p_type,
    p_size;

spool off

connect dss_admin/dss_admin
```

```
set lines 1000
set pages 58
set timing on
ttitle 'Query 14a output'
spool query14a.lst


select
    sum(l_extendedprice) / 7.0 as avg_yearly
from
    lineitem,
    part
where
    p_partkey = l_partkey
    and p_brand = 'Brand#14'
    and p_container = 'SM PACK'
    and l_quantity < (
            select
                    0.2 * avg(l_quantity)
            from
                    lineitem
            where
                    l_partkey = p_partkey
    );

spool off
connect dss_admin/dss_admin
set lines 1000
set pages 58
set timing on
ttitle 'Query 15 output'
spool query15.lst


select
    c_name,
    c_custkey,
    o_orderkey,
    o_orderdate,
    o_totalprice,
    sum(l_quantity)
from
    customer,
    orders,
    lineitem
where
    o_orderkey in (
            select
                    l_orderkey
            from
                    lineitem
            group by
                    l_orderkey having
                            sum(l_quantity) > 314
    )
    and c_custkey = o_custkey
    and o_orderkey = l_orderkey
```

```
          and rownum<101
group by
     c_name,
     c_custkey,
     o_orderkey,
     o_orderdate,
     o_totalprice
order by
     o_totalprice desc,
     o_orderdate;

spool off

connect dss_admin/dss_admin
set lines 1000
set pages 58
set timing on
ttitle 'Query 16 output'
spool query16.lst


select
     sum(l_extendedprice* (1 - l_discount)) revenue
from
     lineitem,
     part
where
     (
             p_partkey = l_partkey
             and p_brand = 'Brand#14'
             and p_container in ('SM CASE', 'SM BOX', 'SM PACK', 'SM
PKG')
             and l_quantity >= 2 and l_quantity <= 2 + 10
             and p_size between 1 and 5
             and l_shipmode in ('AIR', 'AIR REG')
             and l_shipinstruct = 'DELIVER IN PERSON'
     )
     or
     (
             p_partkey = l_partkey
             and p_brand = 'Brand#24'
             and p_container in ('MED BAG', 'MED BOX', 'MED PKG',
'MED PACK')
             and l_quantity >= 12 and l_quantity <= 12 + 10
             and p_size between 1 and 10
             and l_shipmode in ('AIR', 'AIR REG')
             and l_shipinstruct = 'DELIVER IN PERSON'
     )
     or
     (
             p_partkey = l_partkey
             and p_brand = 'Brand#35'
             and p_container in ('LG CASE', 'LG BOX', 'LG PACK', 'LG
PKG')
             and l_quantity >= 28 and l_quantity <= 28 + 10
             and p_size between 1 and 15
             and l_shipmode in ('AIR', 'AIR REG')
```

```
               and l_shipinstruct = 'DELIVER IN PERSON'
     );

spool off

connect dss_admin/dss_admin
set lines 1000
set pages 58
set timing on
ttitle 'Query 17 output'
spool query17.lst


select
     s_name,
     s_address
from
     supplier,
     nation
where
     s_suppkey in (
          select
                    ps_suppkey
          from
                    partsupp
          where
                    ps_partkey in (
                         select
                                   p_partkey
                         from
                                   part
                         where
                                   p_name like 'orange%'
                    )
                    and ps_availqty > (
                         select
                                   0.5 * sum(l_quantity)
                         from
                                   lineitem
                         where
                                   l_partkey = ps_partkey
                                   and l_suppkey = ps_suppkey
                                   and l_shipdate >= to_date( '1994-
01-01','yyyy-mm-dd')
                                   and l_shipdate < date '1994-01-01'
+ interval '1' year
                    )
     )
     and s_nationkey = n_nationkey
     and n_name = 'MOZAMBIQUE'
order by
     s_name;

spool off
connect dss_admin/dss_admin
set lines 1000
set pages 58
```

```
set timing on

ttitle 'Query 18 output'
spool query18.lst


select
    s_name,
    count(*) numwait
from
    supplier,
    lineitem l1,
    orders,
    nation
where
    s_suppkey = l1.l_suppkey
    and o_orderkey = l1.l_orderkey
    and o_orderstatus = 'F'
    and l1.l_receiptdate > l1.l_commitdate
    and exists (
            select
                    *
            from
                    lineitem l2
            where
                    l2.l_orderkey = l1.l_orderkey
                    and l2.l_suppkey <> l1.l_suppkey
    )
    and not exists (
            select
                    *
            from
                    lineitem l3
            where
                    l3.l_orderkey = l1.l_orderkey
                    and l3.l_suppkey <> l1.l_suppkey
                    and l3.l_receiptdate > l3.l_commitdate
    )
    and s_nationkey = n_nationkey
    and n_name = 'GERMANY'
        and rownum<101
group by
    s_name
order by
    numwait desc,
    s_name;

spool off

connect dss_admin/dss_admin
set lines 1000
set pages 58
set timing on
ttitle 'Query 19 output'
spool query19.lst
```

Oracle Solid State Disk Tuning

```
select
    cntrycode,
    count(*) numcust,
    sum(c_acctbal) totacctbal
from
    (
        select
            substr(c_phone, 1, 2) cntrycode,
            c_acctbal
        from
            customer
        where
            substr(c_phone,1,2) in
                ('30', '22', '32', '13', '28', '21',
'24')
            and c_acctbal > (
                select
                    avg(c_acctbal)
                from
                    customer
                where
                    c_acctbal > 0.00
                    and substr(c_phone,1,2) in
                        ('30', '22', '32', '13',
'28', '21', '24')
            )
            and not exists (
                select
                    *
                from
                    orders
                where
                    o_custkey = c_custkey
            )
    ) custsale
group by
    cntrycode
order by
    cntrycode;
select to_char(sysdate,'dd-mon-yyyy hh24:mi') from dual;


spool off
ttitle off
set timing off
```

Example PAR and Data Listings

Appendix B

Appendix B shows the example PAR files (control files) used by the SQL*Loader program to parse the data into the tables. Also provided are the first ten records for each table.

Customer Table

First, an example PAR file used by SQL*Loader to parse the data as it is loaded from the flat file. There were ten of these (1-10) for the customer table for a 20 gigabyte data set.

💾 **File: customer1.par**

```
-- ***************************************************
-- Copyright © 2003 by Rampant TechPress
-- This script is free for non-commercial purposes
-- with no warranties.  Use at your own risk.
--
-- To license this script for a commercial purpose,
-- contact info@rampant.cc
-- ***************************************************

File: customer1.par
load data
infile 'customer.tbl.1'
into table CUSTOMER
fields terminated by '|'
(c_custkey,
c_name,
c_address,
c_nationkey,
c_phone,
c_acctbal,
c_mktsegment,
c_comment)
```

Example Data from customer.tbl.1 (first 10 records):

```
1|Customer#000000001|IVhzIApeRb ot,c,E|15|25-989-741-
2988|711.56|BUILDING|regular, regular platelets are fluffily
according to the even attainments. blithely iron|
2|Customer#000000002|XSTf4,NCwDVaWNe6tEgvwfmRchLXak|13|23-768-687-
3665|121.65|AUTOMOBILE|furiously special deposits solve slyly.
furiously even foxes wake alongside of the furiously ironic ideas.
pending|
3|Customer#000000003|MG9kdTD2WBHm|1|11-719-748-
3364|7498.12|AUTOMOBILE|special packages wake. slyly reg|
4|Customer#000000004|XxVSJsLAGtn|4|14-128-190-
5944|2866.83|MACHINERY|slyly final accounts sublate carefully. slyly
ironic asymptotes nod across the quickly regular pack|
5|Customer#000000005|KvpyuHCplrB84WgAiGV6sYpZq7Tj|3|13-750-942-
6364|794.47|HOUSEHOLD|blithely final instructions haggle; stealthy
sauternes nod; carefully regu|
6|Customer#000000006|sKZz0CsnMD7mp4Xd0YrBvx,LREYKUWAh yVn|20|30-114-
968-4951|7638.57|AUTOMOBILE|special deposits wake along the ironic
foxes. slyly regular deposits are furiously about the blith|
7|Customer#000000007|TcGe5gaZNgVePxU5kRrvXBfkasDTea|18|28-190-982-
9759|9561.95|AUTOMOBILE|theodolites kindle carefully carefully
regular deposits. regular depe|
8|Customer#000000008|I0B10bB0AymmC, 0PrRYBCP1yGJ8xcBPmWhl5|17|27-
147-574-9335|6819.74|BUILDING|ironic deposits are quickly after the
gifts. regular dependencies hinder slyly after the quickly ex|
9|Customer#000000009|xKiAFTjUsCuxfeleNqefumTrjS|8|18-338-906-
3675|8324.07|FURNITURE|deposits affix fluffily. blithely final ideas
are furiously dolphins. i|
10|Customer#000000010|6LrEaV6KR6PLVcgl2ArL Q3rqzLzcT1 v2|5|15-741-
346-9870|2753.54|HOUSEHOLD|bold, final frays sleep carefully special
ideas. carefully final asymptotes sleep furiously against the even
i|
```

Lineitem Table

Next is the *lineitem* table. This is from file lineitem1.par and is 1 of
10 files used to load the 10 flatfiles into the lineitem table.

File: lineitem1.par

```
File: lineitem1.par

load data
infile 'lineitem.tbl.1'
append
into table LINEITEM
append
fields terminated by '|'
(l_orderkey,
l_partkey,
l_suppkey,
l_linenumber,
l_quantity,
l_extendedprice,
l_discount,
l_tax,
l_returnflag,
l_linestatus,
l_shipdate date(10) "YYYY-MM-DD",
l_commitdate date(10) "YYYY-MM-DD",
l_receiptdate date(10) "YYYY-MM-DD",
l_shipinstruct,
l_shipmode,
l_comment)
```

Example Data from lineitem.1.tbl (first 10 records):

```
1|155190|7706|1|17|21168.23|0.04|0.02|N|O|1996-03-13|1996-02-
12|1996-03-22|DELIVER IN PERSON|TRUCK|blithely regular ideas caj|
1|67310|7311|2|36|45983.16|0.09|0.06|N|O|1996-04-12|1996-02-28|1996-
04-20|TAKE BACK RETURN|MAIL|slyly bold pinto beans detect s|
1|63700|3701|3|8|13309.60|0.10|0.02|N|O|1996-01-29|1996-03-05|1996-
01-31|TAKE BACK RETURN|REG AIR|deposits wake furiously dogged,|
1|2132|4633|4|28|28955.64|0.09|0.06|N|O|1996-04-21|1996-03-30|1996-
05-16|NONE|AIR|even ideas haggle. even, bold reque|
1|24027|1534|5|24|22824.48|0.10|0.04|N|O|1996-03-30|1996-03-14|1996-
04-01|NONE|FOB|carefully final gr|
1|15635|638|6|32|49620.16|0.07|0.02|N|O|1996-01-30|1996-02-07|1996-
02-03|DELIVER IN PERSON|MAIL|furiously regular accounts haggle bl|
2|106170|1191|1|38|44694.46|0.00|0.05|N|O|1997-01-28|1997-01-
14|1997-02-02|TAKE BACK RETURN|RAIL|carefully ironic platelets
against t|
3|4297|1798|1|45|54058.05|0.06|0.00|R|F|1994-02-02|1994-01-04|1994-
02-23|NONE|AIR|blithely s|
3|19036|6540|2|49|46796.47|0.10|0.00|R|F|1993-11-09|1993-12-20|1993-
11-24|TAKE BACK RETURN|RAIL|final, regular pinto|
3|128449|3474|3|27|39890.88|0.06|0.07|A|F|1994-01-16|1993-11-
22|1994-01-23|DELIVER IN PERSON|SHIP|carefully silent pinto beans
boost· fur|
```

Orders Table

The orders table was loaded from 10 flatfiles. What follows is orders1.par.

File: orders1.par

```
--  ************************************************
-- Copyright © 2003 by Rampant TechPress
-- This script is free for non-commercial purposes
-- with no warranties.  Use at your own risk.
--
-- To license this script for a commercial purpose,
-- contact info@rampant.cc
--  ************************************************

File: orders1.par

load data
infile 'orders.tbl.1'
into table ORDERS
fields terminated by '|'
(o_orderkey,
o_custkey,
o_orderstatus,
o_totalprice,
o_orderdate date(10) "YYYY-MM-DD",
o_orderpriority,
o_clerk,
o_shippriority,
o_comment)
```

Here are the first ten records from the orders.tbl.1 file:

```
1|36901|O|173665.47|1996-01-02|5-LOW|Clerk#000000951|0|blithely
final dolphins solve-- blithely blithe packages nag blith|
2|78002|O|46929.18|1996-12-01|1-URGENT|Clerk#000000880|0|quickly
regular depend|
3|123314|F|193846.25|1993-10-14|5-LOW|Clerk#000000955|0|deposits
alongside of the dependencies are slowly about |
4|136777|O|32151.78|1995-10-11|5-LOW|Clerk#000000124|0|final
requests detect slyly across the blithely bold pinto beans. eve|
5|44485|F|144659.20|1994-07-30|5-LOW|Clerk#000000925|0|even deposits
cajole furiously. quickly spe|
6|55624|F|58749.59|1992-02-21|4-NOT
SPECIFIED|Clerk#000000058|0|ironically bold asymptotes sleep
blithely beyond the regular, clos|
7|39136|O|252004.18|1996-01-10|2-HIGH|Clerk#000000470|0|ironic,
regular deposits are. ironic foxes sl|
32|130057|O|208660.75|1995-07-16|2-HIGH|Clerk#000000616|0|slyly
final foxes are slyly. packag|
33|66958|F|163243.98|1993-10-27|3-MEDIUM|Clerk#000000409|0|packages
maintain about the deposits; foxes hang after |
34|61001|O|58949.67|1998-07-21|3-MEDIUM|Clerk#000000223|0|quickly
express asymptotes use. carefully final packages sleep f|
```

Part Table

The part table was loaded from 10 flat files using SQL*Loader.
Here is the part1.par file.

🖫 File: part1.par

```
-- ****************************************************
-- Copyright © 2003 by Rampant TechPress
-- This script is free for non-commercial purposes
-- with no warranties.  Use at your own risk.
--
-- To license this script for a commercial purpose,
-- contact info@rampant.cc
-- ****************************************************
File: part1.par
load data
infile 'part.tbl.1'
into table PART
fields terminated by '|'
(p_partkey,
p_name,
p_mfgr,
p_brand,
p_type,
p_size,
```

```
p_container,
p_retailprice,
p_comment)
```

Here are the first ten rows of data from the part.tbl.1 flat file:

```
1|goldenrod lace spring peru powder|Manufacturer#1|Brand#13|PROMO
BURNISHED COPPER|7|JUMBO PKG|901.00|final deposits s|
2|blush rosy metallic lemon navajo|Manufacturer#1|Brand#13|LARGE
BRUSHED BRASS|1|LG CASE|902.00|final platelets hang f|
3|dark green antique puff wheat|Manufacturer#4|Brand#42|STANDARD
POLISHED BRASS|21|WRAP CASE|903.00|unusual excuses ac|
4|chocolate metallic smoke ghost drab|Manufacturer#3|Brand#34|SMALL
PLATED BRASS|14|MED DRUM|904.00|ironi|
5|forest blush chiffon thistle
chocolate|Manufacturer#3|Brand#32|STANDARD POLISHED TIN|15|SM
PKG|905.00|pending, spe|
6|white ivory azure firebrick black|Manufacturer#2|Brand#24|PROMO
PLATED STEEL|4|MED BAG|906.00|pending pinto be|
7|blue blanched tan indian olive|Manufacturer#1|Brand#11|SMALL
PLATED COPPER|45|SM BAG|907.00|blithely ironic|
8|ivory khaki cream midnight rosy|Manufacturer#4|Brand#44|PROMO
BURNISHED TIN|41|LG DRUM|908.00|furiously eve|
9|thistle rose moccasin light floral|Manufacturer#4|Brand#43|SMALL
BURNISHED STEEL|12|WRAP CASE|909.00|thinly even request|
10|floral moccasin royal powder
burnished|Manufacturer#5|Brand#54|LARGE BURNISHED STEEL|44|LG
CAN|910.01|bold, ironic |
```

Partsupp Table

The partsupp table was loaded from 10 flatfiles using SQL*Loader. The following is file partsupp1.par used to parse the data by SQL*Loader.

💾 **File: partsupp1.par**

```
-- ***************************************************
-- Copyright © 2003 by Rampant TechPress
-- This script is free for non-commercial purposes
-- with no warranties.  Use at your own risk.
--
-- To license this script for a commercial purpose,
-- contact info@rampant.cc
-- ***************************************************
File: partsupp1.par
load data
infile 'partsupp.tbl.1'
into table PARTSUPP
```

```
fields terminated by '|'
(ps_partkey,
ps_suppkey,
ps_availqty,
ps_supplycost,
ps_comment)
```

Here are the first ten records from the partsupp.tbl.1 file:

```
1|2|3325|771.64|requests after the carefully ironic ideas cajole
alongside of the enticingly special accounts. fluffily regular
deposits haggle about the blithely ironic deposits. regular requests
sleep c|
1|2502|8076|993.49|careful pinto beans wake slyly furiously silent
pinto beans. accounts wake pendi|
1|5002|3956|337.09|boldly silent requests detect. quickly regular
courts are. instructions haggle ironic foxes. sometimes final orbits
cajole fluffily around the unusual foxes. slyly silent theodolites
cajole r|
1|7502|4069|357.84|regular deposits are. furiously even packages
cajole furiously. even pinto beans boost furiously final
dependencies. f|
2|3|8895|378.49|furiously even asymptotes are furiously regular
plate|
2|2503|4969|915.27|even accounts wake furiously. idle instructions
sleep in |
2|5003|8539|438.37|furiously even pinto beans serve about the ironic
idea|
2|7503|3025|306.39|deposits according to the final, special foxes
detec|
3|4|4651|920.92|ironic, pending theodolites sleep slyly at the slyly
final foxes. slyly ironic accounts sleep express accounts. quickly
fina|
3|2504|4093|498.13|furiously final requests nag after the even
instructions. quickly pending accounts with the ironic packages
sleep quickly blithely |
3|5004|3917|645.40|ideas along the fluffily special deposits detect
furiously furiously quiet attainments. slyly special theodolites
affix among the furiously bold dolphins. slyly final |
```

Region Table

The region table was loaded from one flat file. The following is the region.par file used to parse the data by SQL*Loader.

File: region.par

```
-- **************************************************
-- Copyright © 2003 by Rampant TechPress
-- This script is free for non-commercial purposes
-- with no warranties.  Use at your own risk.
--
-- To license this script for a commercial purpose,
-- contact info@rampant.cc
-- **************************************************

File: region.par
load data
infile 'region.tbl'
into table REGION
fields terminated by '|'
(r_regionkey,r_name,r_comment)
```

Here are the records in the region.tbl flat file:

```
0|AFRICA|special Tiresias about the furiously even dolphins are
furi|
1|AMERICA|even, ironic theodolites according to the bold platelets
wa|
2|ASIA|silent, bold requests sleep slyly across the quickly sly
dependencies. furiously silent instructions alongside |
3|EUROPE|special, bold deposits haggle foxes. platelet|
4|MIDDLE EAST|furiously unusual packages use carefully above the
unusual, exp|
```

Supplier Table

The supplier table was loaded from 10 flatfiles. The following is from the supplier1.par file used by SQL*Loader to parse the flatfiles during the load.

File: supplier1.par

```
-- **************************************************
-- Copyright © 2003 by Rampant TechPress
-- This script is free for non-commercial purposes
-- with no warranties.  Use at your own risk.
--
-- To license this script for a commercial purpose,
-- contact info@rampant.cc
-- **************************************************
File: supplier1.par
```

```
load data
infile 'supplier.tbl.1'
into table SUPPLIER
fields terminated by '|'
(s_suppkey,
s_name,
s_address,
s_nationkey,
s_phone,
s_acctbal,
s_comment)
```

Here are the first 10 records from the supplier.tbl.1 flat file:

```
1|Supplier#000000001| N kD4on9OM Ipw3,gf0JBoQDd7tgrzrddZ|17|27-918-
335-1736|5755.94|requests haggle carefully. accounts sublate
finally. carefully ironic pa|
2|Supplier#000000002|89eJ5ksX3ImxJQBvxObC,|5|15-679-861-
2259|4032.68|furiously stealthy frays thrash alongside of the slyly
express deposits. blithely regular req|
3|Supplier#000000003|q1,G3Pj6OjIuUYfUoH18BFTKP5aU9bEV3|1|11-383-516-
1199|4192.40|furiously regular instructions impress slyly! carefu|
4|Supplier#000000004|Bk7ah4CK8SYQTepEmvMkkgMwg|15|25-843-787-
7479|4641.08|final ideas cajole. furiously close dep|
5|Supplier#000000005|Gcdm2rJRzl5qlTVzc|11|21-151-690-3663|-
283.84|carefully silent instructions are slyly according t|
6|Supplier#000000006|tQxuVm7s7CnK|14|24-696-997-4969|1365.79|even
requests wake carefully! fluffily final pinto beans run slyly among
t|
7|Supplier#000000007|s,4TicNGB4uO6PaSqNBUq|23|33-990-965-
2201|6820.35|carefully express packages believe furiously after the
fur|
8|Supplier#000000008|9Sq4bBH2FQEmaFOocY45sRTxo6yuoG|17|27-498-742-
3860|7627.85|carefully express escapades are slyly |
9|Supplier#000000009|1KhUgZegwM3ua7dsYmekYBsK|10|20-403-398-
8662|5302.37|slyly regular decoys mold slyly ironic dugouts.
requests are carefully-- carefully|
10|Supplier#000000010|Saygah3gYWMp72i PY|24|34-852-489-
8585|3891.91|ironic deposits poach quickly furiously final accounts.
carefull|
```

Nation Table

The nation table was loaded from one flat file. The following is
the nation.par file used by the SQL*Loader program to parse the
records during loading.

```
-- **************************************************
-- Copyright © 2003 by Rampant TechPress
-- This script is free for non-commercial purposes
-- with no warranties.  Use at your own risk.
--
-- To license this script for a commercial purpose,
-- contact info@rampant.cc
-- **************************************************
File: nation.par
load data
infile 'nation.tbl'
into table NATION
fields terminated by '|'
(n_nationkey,n_name,n_regionkey,n_comment)
```

Here are the records from the nation.tbl flat file:

```
0|ALGERIA|0|final accounts wake quickly. special reques|
1|ARGENTINA|1|idly final instructions cajole stealthily. regular
instructions wake carefully blithely express accounts. fluffi|
2|BRAZIL|1|always pending pinto beans sleep sil|
3|CANADA|1|foxes among the bold requests|
4|EGYPT|4|pending accounts haggle furiously. furiously bold accounts
detect. platelets at the packages haggle caref|
5|ETHIOPIA|0|fluffily ruthless requests integrate fluffily. pending
ideas wake blithely acco|
6|FRANCE|3|even requests detect near the pendin|
7|GERMANY|3|blithely ironic foxes grow. quickly pending accounts are
b|
8|INDIA|2|ironic packages should have to are slyly around the
special, ironic accounts. iron|
9|INDONESIA|2|unusual excuses are quickly requests. slyly ironic
accounts haggle carefully above the pendin|
10|IRAN|4|blithely even accounts about the furiously regular foxes
nag slyly final accounts. quickly final fo|
11|IRAQ|4|express, pending deposits boost quick|
12|JAPAN|2|blithely final packages cajole quickly even dependencies?
blithely regular deposits haggle express, ironic re|
13|JORDAN|4|blithe, express deposits boost carefully busy accounts.
furiously pending depos|
14|KENYA|0|ironic requests boost. quickly pending pinto beans cajole
slyly slyly even deposits. ironic packages |
15|MOROCCO|0|ideas according to the fluffily final pinto beans sleep
furiously|
16|MOZAMBIQUE|0|ironic courts wake fluffily even, bold deposi|
17|PERU|1|final, final accounts sleep slyly across the requests. |
18|CHINA|2|bold accounts are. slyly ironic escapades haggle acc|
19|ROMANIA|3|deposits boost against the brave id|
20|SAUDI ARABIA|4|fluffily final accounts wake slyly-- fi|
21|VIETNAM|2|doggedly ironic requests haggle furiously ironic,
ironic packages. furiously final courts wake fur|
```

22|RUSSIA|3|slowly pending patterns x-ray quickly. ironic, even
accounts haggle furiously. even, final deposits mold bl|
23|UNITED KINGDOM|3|fluffily regular pinto beans breach according to
the ironic dolph|
24|UNITED STATES|1|blithely regular deposits serve furiously
blithely regular warthogs! slyly fi|

Data Loading and Index Build Statistics

Appendix C

This appendix contains the raw load and index build statistics tables for the tests.

Load Statistics for the Solid State Array

SSD Load File	Rows	Seconds	Rows/sec	CPU Sec	Comp to ATA
customer1	300000	8.60	34883.72	3.09	0.766
customer2	300000	8.87	33821.87	3.05	0.761
customer3	300000	9.06	33112.58	2.99	0.766
customer4	300000	8.90	33707.87	3.34	0.749
customer5	300000	8.42	35629.45	2.96	0.705
customer6	300000	8.57	35005.83	2.76	0.711
customer7	300000	8.34	35971.22	2.9	0.647
customer8	300000	8.36	35885.17	2.93	0.683
customer9	300000	8.64	34722.22	2.93	0.724
customer10	300000	8.29	36188.18	2.88	0.523
lineitem1	11997996	589.67	20346.97	159.7	0.614
lineitem2	11998608	579.27	20713.33	160.14	0.748
lineitem3	12003544	582.77	20597.40	162.86	0.733
lineitem4	11988859	582.29	20589.15	160.66	0.745
lineitem5	11997045	585.92	20475.57	162.52	0.756
lineitem6	11999025	587.02	20440.57	163.7	0.755
lineitem7	12003017	591.99	20275.71	159.66	0.755
lineitem8	12000546	590.59	20319.59	158.65	0.738
lineitem9	12000642	593.44	20222.17	157.38	0.752
lineitem10	12005326	595.07	20174.64	159.57	0.756

SSD					
Load File	Rows	Seconds	Rows/sec	CPU Sec	Comp to ATA
nation	25	0.07	357.14	0	1.400
order1	3000000	129.32	23198.27	27.68	0.824
order2	3000000	128.86	23281.08	28.47	0.696
order3	3000000	132.46	22648.35	27.93	0.836
order4	3000000	131.77	22766.94	28.44	0.700
order5	3000000	131.65	22787.69	27.4	0.816
order6	3000000	130.91	22916.51	28.52	0.696
order7	3000000	133.60	22455.09	27.5	0.816
order8	3000000	133.40	22488.76	28.42	0.704
order9	3000000	133.93	22399.76	28.11	0.811
order10	3000000	137.52	21815.01	27.47	0.711
part1	400000	15.01	26648.90	3.95	0.562
part2	400000	14.97	26720.11	3.68	0.554
part3	400000	15.26	26212.32	3.99	0.592
part4	400000	15.16	26385.22	4.11	0.753
part5	400000	15.41	25957.17	3.94	0.780
part6	400000	15.75	25396.83	3.88	0.800
part7	400000	16.45	24316.11	3.75	0.825
part8	400000	16.46	24301.34	3.76	0.826
part9	400000	16.35	24464.83	3.42	0.820
part10	400000	15.81	25300.44	3.9	0.783
partsupp1	1600000	51.58	31019.78	12.82	0.560
partsupp2	1600000	52.88	30257.19	12.09	0.605
partsupp3	1600000	53.53	29889.78	12.87	0.707
partsupp4	1600000	52.47	30493.62	12.63	0.513
partsupp5	1600000	54.88	29154.52	12.89	0.674
partsupp6	1600000	54.43	29395.55	12.76	0.688
partsupp7	1600000	52.94	30222.89	12.91	0.506
partsupp8	1600000	55.56	28797.70	12.77	0.722
partsupp9	1600000	53.13	30114.81	12.66	0.629
partsupp10	1600000	53.39	29968.16	13.55	0.516
region	5	0.12	41.67	0.01	1.500
supplier1	20000	0.64	31250.00	0.22	0.762
supplier2	20000	0.54	37037.04	0.14	0.720
supplier3	20000	0.66	30303.03	0.23	0.759
supplier4	20000	0.61	32786.89	0.19	0.735

SSD

Load File	Rows	Seconds	Rows/sec	CPU Sec	Comp to ATA
supplier5	20000	0.57	35087.72	0.18	0.722
supplier6	20000	0.59	33898.31	0.23	0.728
supplier7	20000	0.56	35714.29	0.17	0.727
supplier8	20000	0.54	37037.04	0.19	0.643
supplier9	20000	0.55	36363.64	0.18	0.611
supplier10	20000	0.75	26666.67	0.14	0.949

Load Data for the ATA Array

SCSI

File	Rows	Hrs	Mins	Secs	Total Secs	Rows/ Sec	Comp to SSD
customer1.log	300000	0.00	0.00	11.22	11.220	26737.97	1.304651
customer2.log	300000	0.00	0.00	11.66	11.660	25728.99	1.314543
customer3.log	300000	0.00	0.00	11.83	11.830	25359.26	1.30574
customer4.log	300000	0.00	0.00	11.88	11.880	25252.53	1.334831
customer5.log	300000	0.00	0.00	11.95	11.950	25104.60	1.41924
customer6.log	300000	0.00	0.00	12.05	12.050	24896.27	1.406068
customer7.log	300000	0.00	0.00	12.89	12.890	23273.86	1.545564
customer8.log	300000	0.00	0.00	12.24	12.240	24509.80	1.464115
customer9.log	300000	0.00	0.00	11.93	11.930	25146.69	1.380787
customer10.log	300000	0.00	0.00	15.85	15.850	18927.44	1.911942
lineitem1.log	11997996	0.00	16.00	0.52	960.520	12491.15	1.628911
lineitem2.log	11998608	0.00	12.00	54.62	774.620	15489.67	1.337235
lineitem3.log	12003544	0.00	13.00	14.76	794.760	15103.36	1.363763
lineitem4.log	11988859	0.00	13.00	2.03	782.030	15330.43	1.343025
lineitem5.log	11997045	0.00	12.00	54.7	774.700	15486.05	1.322194
lineitem6.log	11999025	0.00	12.00	57.7	777.700	15428.86	1.324827
lineitem7.log	12003017	0.00	13.00	4.35	784.350	15303.14	1.324938
lineitem8.log	12000546	0.00	13.00	20.35	800.350	14994.12	1.35517
lineitem9.log	12000642	0.00	13.00	8.78	788.780	15214.18	1.329166
lineitem10.log	12005326	0.00	13.00	7.21	787.210	15250.47	1.322886
nation.log	25	0.00	0.00	0.05	0.050	500.00	0.714286
order1.log	3000000	0.00	2.00	36.9	156.900	19120.46	1.213269
order2.log	3000000	0.00	3.00	5.15	185.150	16203.08	1.436831
order3.log	3000000	0.00	2.00	38.46	158.460	18932.22	1.196286

order4.log	3000000	0.00	3.00	8.24	188.240	15937.10	1.42855
order5.log	3000000	0.00	2.00	41.34	161.340	18594.27	1.225522
order6.log	3000000	0.00	3.00	8.21	188.210	15939.64	1.437705
order7.log	3000000	0.00	2.00	43.76	163.760	18319.49	1.225749
order8.log	3000000	0.00	3.00	9.62	189.620	15821.12	1.421439
order9.log	3000000	0.00	2.00	45.1	165.100	18170.81	1.232734
order10.log	3000000	0.00	3.00	13.42	193.420	15510.29	1.406486
part1.log	400000	0.00	0.00	26.7	26.700	14981.27	1.778814
part2.log	400000	0.00	0.00	27.04	27.040	14792.90	1.806279
part3.log	400000	0.00	0.00	25.77	25.770	15521.92	1.688729
part4.log	400000	0.00	0.00	20.12	20.120	19880.72	1.327177
part5.log	400000	0.00	0.00	19.75	19.750	20253.16	1.281635
part6.log	400000	0.00	0.00	19.69	19.690	20314.88	1.250159
part7.log	400000	0.00	0.00	19.95	19.950	20050.13	1.212766
part8.log	400000	0.00	0.00	19.92	19.920	20080.32	1.210207
part9.log	400000	0.00	0.00	19.93	19.930	20070.25	1.21896
part10.log	400000	0.00	0.00	20.2	20.200	19801.98	1.277672
partsupp1.log	1600000	0.00	1.00	32.16	92.160	17361.11	1.786739
partsupp2.log	1600000	0.00	1.00	27.34	87.340	18319.21	1.651664
partsupp3.log	1600000	0.00	1.00	15.67	75.670	21144.44	1.4136
partsupp4.log	1600000	0.00	1.00	42.31	102.310	15638.74	1.949876
partsupp5.log	1600000	0.00	1.00	21.41	81.410	19653.61	1.483418
partsupp6.log	1600000	0.00	1.00	19.07	79.070	20235.23	1.452692
partsupp7.log	1600000	0.00	1.00	44.7	104.700	15281.76	1.977711
partsupp8.log	1600000	0.00	1.00	16.98	76.980	20784.62	1.385529
partsupp9.log	1600000	0.00	1.00	24.48	84.480	18939.39	1.590062
partsupp10.log	1600000	0.00	1.00	43.44	103.440	15467.90	1.937441
region.log	5	0.00	0.00	0.08	0.080	62.50	0.666667
supplier1.log	20000	0.00	0.00	0.84	0.840	23809.52	1.3125
supplier2.log	20000	0.00	0.00	0.75	0.750	26666.67	1.388889
supplier3.log	20000	0.00	0.00	0.87	0.870	22988.51	1.318182
supplier4.log	20000	0.00	0.00	0.83	0.830	24096.39	1.360656
supplier5.log	20000	0.00	0.00	0.79	0.790	25316.46	1.385965
supplier6.log	20000	0.00	0.00	0.81	0.810	24691.36	1.372881
supplier7.log	20000	0.00	0.00	0.77	0.770	25974.03	1.375
supplier8.log	20000	0.00	0.00	0.84	0.840	23809.52	1.555556
supplier9.log	20000	0.00	0.00	0.9	0.900	22222.22	1.636364
supplier10.log	20000	0.00	0.00	0.79	0.790	25316.46	1.053333

Index Creation Data

Table	Row Count	Index	Column	SSD Build Time	SCSI Build Time	SSD/ ATA Ratio	ATA/ SSD Ratio
Customer	3000000	cust_mktseg	customer (c_mktsegment)	16	28	0.5714	1.7500
Customer	3000000	cust_nk	customer (c_nationkey)	15	24	0.6250	1.6000
Lineitem	119994608	lineitem_ok	lineitem (l_orderkey)	460	661	0.6959	1.4370
Lineitem	119994608	lineitem_prtk	lineitem(l_partkey)	828	1199	0.6906	1.4481
Lineitem	119994608	lineitem_sd	lineitem (l_shipdate)	874	1318	0.6631	1.5080
Lineitem	119994608	lineitem_si	lineitem (l_shipinstruct)	811	976	0.8309	1.2035
Lineitem	119994608	lineitem_sm	lineitem (l_shipmode)	696	1047	0.6648	1.5043
Lineitem	119994608	lineitem_supk	lineitem (l_suppkey)	822	1195	0.6879	1.4538
Orders	30000000	orders_odat	orders (o_orderdate)	201	298	0.6745	1.4826
Part	4000000	part_brd	part(p_brand)	12	33	0.3636	2.7500
Part	4000000	part_con	part(p_container)	21	23	0.9130	1.0952
Part	4000000	part_sz	part(p_size)	20	22	0.9091	1.1000
Part	4000000	part_typ	part(p_type)	25	28	0.8929	1.1200
Partsupp	16000000	partsupp_sk	partsupp (ps_suppkey)	60	88	0.6818	1.4667
Suppliers	200000	supp_nk	supplier (s_nationkey)	1	2	0.5000	2.0000
Total/avg				4862	6942	0.6910	1.5279
Hours				1.3506	1.9283		

STATSPACK Report Listings

Appendix D

This appendix contains the example STATSPACK reports. Some of the reports have been edited to exclude client specific information.

SSD Query Run Results

SSD query	Run1	Run2	Run3	Run4	Run5	Run6	Run7
1	589.94	501.53	502.47	500.54	501.06	507.31	615.21
2	42.24	30.83	30.76	30.44	30.37	30.55	43.18
3	41.55	34.72	35.54	34.83	35.49	35.35	40.86
4	249.30	139.02	139.30	139.42	42.04	136.11	267.70
5	292.28	161.48	162.43	160.54	161.17	158.40	317.08
6	205.12	107.87	109.20	108.88	108.78	107.37	230.25
7	314.09	161.59	162.83	162.01	162.14	156.74	334.97
7a	263.43	144.45	145.12	145.42	144.85	139.88	297.13
8	340.17	272.98	274.20	273.95	273.32	267.27	379.45
9	137.69	137.40	138.78	137.62	138.40	134.25	154.53
10	35.20	35.46	35.72	35.51	35.49	35.28	36.19
11	157.74	159.13	161.64	161.27	160.43	154.48	160.75
12	224.77	215.71	217.33	214.72	215.66	214.58	225.20
13	113.01	113.16	113.79	113.76	113.93	111.85	114.70
13a	246.45	248.79	250.66	249.36	250.39	238.84	249.17
14	57.98	44.32	42.82	41.95	42.04	42.19	54.56
14a	42.49	40.66	40.91	40.50	40.34	50.65	39.86
15	309.07	306.37	308.89	306.73	306.27	305.89	307.92
16	138.37	138.70	140.02	138.65	139.12	565.86	138.11
17	133.08	133.53	134.41	133.71	133.36	355.08	132.71
18	149.93	150.41	150.93	150.86	150.56	319.14	149.90

SSD query	Run1	Run2	Run3	Run4	Run5	Run6	Run7
19	43.58	44.03	44.44	43.41	43.19	47.45	43.35
Total	4127.48	3322.14	3342.19	3324.08	3228.40	4114.52	4332.78

SCSI/ATA Query Results

ATA query	Run1	Run2	Run3	Run4	Run5
1	86400.00	86400.00	86400.00	86400.00	86400.00
2	207.62	161.84	162.90	165.08	358.03
3	0.00	86400.00	86400.00	12657.46	4317.06
4	4313.82	3666.76	3372.94	243.31	228.24
5	13568.08	17804.46	0.00	2145.11	1912.33
6	61926.08	61367.15	61547.58	4823.09	4581.85
7	133456.46	132743.60	86400.00	23259.28	22497.74
7a	33038.67	40758.41	41817.98	13807.28	4158.16
8	36062.61	46331.87	284.91	5361.54	8134.71
9	4779.68	5138.53	86400.00	1550.05	406.09
10	6125.83	9278.53	5544.37	1164.96	347.61
11	1650.96	1144.37	62632.58	5602.72	8191.45
12	249.64	319.86	0.00	300.85	256.31
13	86400.00	86400.00	5283.60	444.54	457.22
13a	86400.00	86400.00	86400.00	86400.00	131326.99
14	106.79	75.49	0.00	94.00	86.51
14a	917.28	1323.80	1228.10	154.44	108.91
15	2803.80	1511.22	0.00	1205.10	690.55
16	1958.00	2309.16	1909.33	662.30	519.49
17	65826.95	66631.73	86400.00	10388.28	7947.97
18	118.65	86400.00	86400.00	4597.52	3471.07
19	120.06	222.30	108.98	49.91	46.28
Total Sec	626430.98	822789.08	788693.27	261476.82	286444.57
Total Days	7.25	9.52	9.13	3.03	3.32

Oracle Solid State Disk Tuning

Index

About Donald Burleson

Don Burleson is one of the world's top Oracle Database experts with more than 20 years of full-time DBA experience. He specializes in creating database architectures for very large online databases and he has worked with some of the world's most powerful and complex systems.

A former Adjunct Professor, Don Burleson has written 32 books, published more than 100 articles in National Magazines, and serves as Editor-in-Chief of Oracle Internals and Senior Consulting Editor for DBAZine and Series Editor for Rampant TechPress. Don is a popular lecturer and teacher and is a frequent speaker at OracleWorld and other international database conferences.

As a leading corporate database consultant, Don has worked with numerous Fortune 500 corporations creating robust database architectures for mission-critical systems. Don is also a noted expert on eCommerce systems, and has been instrumental in the development of numerous Web-based systems that support thousands of concurrent users.

In addition to his services as a consultant, Don also is active in charitable programs to aid visually impaired individuals. Don pioneered a technique for delivering tiny pigmy horses as guide animals for the blind and manages a non-profit corporation called the Guide Horse Foundation dedicated to providing Guide horses to blind people free-of-charge. The Web Site for The Guide Horse Foundation is www.guidehorse.org.

About Mike Ault

Mike Ault is one of the leading names in Oracle technology. The author of more than 20 Oracle books and hundreds of articles in national publications, Mike Ault has five Oracle Masters Certificates and was the first popular Oracle author with his landmark book "Oracle7 Administration and Management". Mike also wrote several of the "Exam Cram" books, and enjoys a reputation as a leading author and Oracle consultant.

Mike started working with computers in 1979 right out of a stint in the Nuclear Navy. He began working with Oracle in 1990 and has since become a World Renowned Oracle expert. Mike is currently a Senior Technical Management Consultant and has two wonderful daughters. Mike is kept out of trouble by his wife of 29 years, Susan.

About Mike Reed

When he first started drawing, Mike Reed drew just to amuse himself. It wasn't long, though, before he knew he wanted to be an artist. Today he does illustrations for children's books, magazines, catalogs, and ads.

He also teaches illustration at the College of Visual Art in St. Paul, Minnesota. Mike Reed says, "Making pictures is like acting — you can paint yourself into the action." He often paints on the computer, but he also draws in pen and ink and paints in acrylics. He feels that learning to draw well is the key to being a successful artist.

Mike is regarded as one of the nation's premier illustrators and is the creator of the popular "Flame Warriors" illustrations at **www.flamewarriors.com**, a website devoted to Internet insults. "To enter his Flame Warriors site is sort of like entering a hellish Sesame Street populated by Oscar the Grouch and 83 of his relatives." – Los Angeles Times. (http://redwing.hutman.net/%7Emreed/warriorshtm/lat.htm)

Mike Reed has always enjoyed reading. As a young child, he liked the Dr. Seuss books. Later, he started reading biographies and war stories. One reason why he feels lucky to be an illustrator is because he can listen to books on tape while he works. Mike is available to provide custom illustrations for all manner of publications at reasonable prices. Mike can be reached at **www.mikereedillustration.com**.

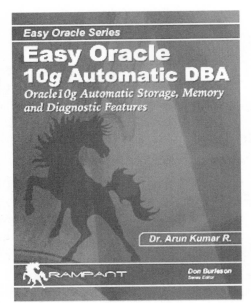

Easy Oracle 10g Automatic DBA

Oracle10g Automatic Storage, Memory and Diagnostic Features

By: Dr. Arun Kumar R.

ISBN 0-9745993-6-0
Retail Price $27.95 / £17.95

This indispensable book shows how a non-Oracle person can quickly install and configure Oracle database 10g for automatic database administration. In less than a day, you can have a complete ready-to-use Oracle database.

Written by one of the world's leading Oracle technology experts, Professor Kumar targets his insights into this highly pragmatic book. This book explains how to use the powerful Oracle 10g automatic features for simple database administration. It has complete coverage for 10g Automatic Storage Management (ASM), 10g Automatic Workload Repository (AWR), Automatic Database Diagnostic Monitor (ADDM), Automatic SGA Management (ASM) and the SQL Tuning Advisor.

For practicing Oracle professionals, this book has a special "for gurus" section at the end of each chapter where Dr. Kumar explains the new Oracle10g v$ views and exposes the internal mechanisms behind these automatic tuning and configuration tools.

http://www.rampant-books.com

Oracle Dataguard

Standby Database Failover Handbook

By: Bipul Kumar

ISBN 0-9745993-8-7
Retail Price $27.95 / £19.95

This book is an essential guide for planning a disaster recovery strategy. Covering all areas of disaster recovery, standby database and automatic Oracle failover, this book explains how the use of Oracle10g Data Guard provides a comprehensive solution for disaster recovery. This book covers all aspects of Oracle Data Guard in detail and provides an overview of the latest Data Guard features in Oracle10g.

Written by a working Oracle DBA, this text covers the concepts and the architecture of standby databases and provides a detailed description of the implementation and management of data guard. Expert tips are revealed for success in configuration and first-time implementation of Data Guard. Advance topics such as "Using RMAN to create Data Guard Configuration" and "Data Guard Broker" have been explained in detail to assist production DBAs managing multiple databases.

http://www.rampant-books.com

Oracle Performance Troubleshooting

with Dictionary Internals SQL & Tuning Scripts

Robin Schumacher

ISBN 0-9727513-4-3
Retail Price $27.95 / £17.95

If you're a DBA who's looking for real world Oracle tuning techniques, Oracle scripts, and advice on how to get to the heart of critical Oracle performance problems, then you've come to the right place. Written by one the world's top DBAs and Oracle internals experts, Robin Schumacher focuses his incredible knowledge of the Oracle data dictionary into a superb book that shows how to quickly troubleshoot and correct Oracle performance problems.

As a Vice President at Embarcadero Technologies, Robin Schumacher has written the internals for some of the world's most powerful Oracle performance software and now he shows you how to use the most recent advancements in Oracle8i and 9i to make your Oracle database run as fast as possible.

http://www.rampant-books.com

Oracle Streams

High Speed Replication and Data Sharing

Madhu Tumma

ISBN 0-9745993-5-2
Retail Price $16.95 / £10.95

Oracle Streams is a high-speed tool that allows synchronization of replicated databases across the globe. It is an indispensable feature for any company using Oracle for global eCommerce. A noted and respected Oracle author, Madhu Tumma, shares his secrets for achieving high-speed replication and data sharing. Using proven techniques from mission-critical application, Tumma show the front-line secrets for ensuring success with Oracle Streams. From installation through implementation, Tumma provides step-by-step instruction to ensure success with these powerful Oracle features.

Tumma walks you safely through the myriad of complex Oracle Streams tasks including the set-up of the staging area queue, propagation through data hubs, customized apply functions, rule-based data propagation, Oracle Streams transformation, and lots, lots more. Best of all, Tumma shares working code examples that allow easy management of even the most complex Oracle Streams implementation.

http://www.rampant-books.com

Free!

Oracle 10g Senior DBA Reference Poster

This 24 x 36 inch quick reference includes the important data columns and relationships between the DBA views, allowing you to quickly write complex data dictionary queries.

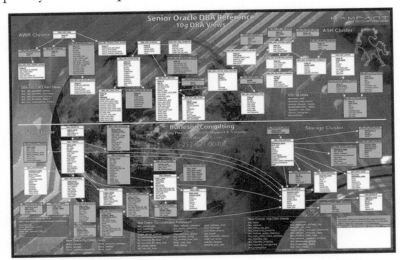

This comprehensive data dictionary reference contains the most important columns from the most important Oracle10g DBA views. Especially useful are the Automated Workload Repository (AWR) and Active Session History (ASH) DBA views.

WARNING - This poster is not suitable for beginners. It is designed for senior Oracle DBAs and requires knowledge of Oracle data dictionary internal structures. You can get your poster at this URL:

www.rampant.cc/poster.htm